LANCASHIRE & YORKSHIRE RAILWAY Miscellany

by Noel Coates

Oxford Publishing Co.

ISBN 86093 188 9

Frontispiece
Having seen thousands of L&Y photographs, this remains my favourite, showing two of the most famous locomotive classes in full cry. The reason for this double-heading is, alas, an imbalance in the new LMS timetable. Although taken in 1924 this Manchester to York express, near Middleton Junction, is pure L&Y.

The late G. W. Smith

Typesetting by Aquarius Typesetting Services, New Milton, Hants.

Printed in Great Britain by
Biddles Ltd, Guildford, Surrey

Published by:
Oxford Publishing Company,
Link House,
West Street,
POOLE, Dorset

INTRODUCTION

The L&Y was the epitome of northern industrial life; that conjunction of toil, honesty, 'down to earth' ruggedness and no nonsense that existed until the depression of the 1930s and, in this 'Miscellany', I have set out to illustrate that character. I have tried to illustrate as many aspects of the Lancashire & Yorkshire Railway as possible, not just the locomotives, but to say a little of what the Railway was and what made it tick; its practices, foibles and eccentricities, its shortcomings and innovations and that glorious Edwardian faith in the future. I have also attempted to show some of the changes which took place in the 60 years from 1860 to 1920. Inevitably some items have had to be left out, even personal favourites, but the major facets have been covered and new material photographed by the L&Y itself has made it possible to create several feature sections, throwing extra light on important aspects of the Company's history. These are specifically, electrification, the Great War and early locomotives (many of which, surprisingly, ran in Aspinall's days), featured in a section entitled 'The Middle Years'.

The limited amount of space available has forced the use of many abbreviations, the majority of which have a conventional acceptance. In contrast, I have tried, wherever possible, to use the terms and nomenclature of the L&Y and its historical period, hence, what we now call the First World War was then known as the Great War and has been termed such. Within the captions, reference to 'break' and 'brake' vans occur. It has been necessary to differ the spelling depending on the photograph to which the caption applies, as it was not until after the Great War that the spelling 'brake' was adopted.

Creating this book has given me immense pleasure and in its preparation I have been very fortunate to have received the help and advice of many old friends and, at the same time, make new friendships as people have lent photographs or offered information. Principal amongst these long-standing friends who have allowed me extensive use of their collections are several members of the Lancashire & Yorkshire Railway Society, and I owe the greatest debt of gratitude to Messrs. P. Gibb, J. B. Hodgson, B. C. Lane and T. Wray. Other Society members who have helped are Messrs. E. Blakey, G. Foxley, R. J. Hunter, M. Oates, J. Peden, R. Stansfield, S. Sutcliffe and A. Wilkinson. From the LMS Society Messrs. V. R. Anderson, R. J. Essery, D. F. Tee and H. N. Twells have loaned material from their collections whilst two more very old friends, now no longer Society members, who have also helped with photographs, are Messrs. A. G. Ellis and F. W. Shuttleworth. To all of you I express my gratitude. Several of the above-named have also loaned photographs taken by those late enthusiasts who knew, loved and photographed the Railway in its prime and a great debt is owed by us all to Messrs. E. Mason, G. W. Smith, J. M. Tomlinson and W. H. Whitworth. I must also thank Mr J. M. Kay of the Blackpool Locomotive Fund, and Lakeside Railway Society for permission to use pictures from the B. H. Ellston collection. Finally, and possibly most importantly, I have to thank the Keeper and staff of the National Railway Museum, and in particular Mr J. Edgington, for permission to use photographs from the official collection which were actually taken for the L&Y itself from about 1895 to 1923. Others who have given advice, help and encouragement and who I must also thank are Messrs. T. Beckett, T. Foley, T. T. Sutcliffe and N. Ward. If I have inadvertently omitted anyone who has, in any way, helped, I apologise now.

The Lancashire & Yorkshire Railway Society exists to join together all those interested in any aspect of the Company's history. Details are available from the secretary, T. Wray, 30 Mossway, Middleton, Greater Manchester, M24 1NS.

Finally, I must admit to having a Lancastrian's bias towards the Railway, but a Yorkshireman may well have another viewpoint of one of the few things, the Lancashire & Yorkshire Railway, ever to unite the two counties.

Noel G. Coates

Typical of L&Y direction notices is this one from Mytholmroyd Station.

V. R. Anderson

LANCASHIRE AND YORKSHIRE RAILWAY

BALTIC PORTS
STETTIN
HAMBURG
BREMEN
DELFZIEL
HARLINGEN
AMSTERDAM
ROTTERDAM
ANTWERP
GHENT
BRUGES
ZEEBRUGGE
DUNKIRK
BOULOGNE
AND OTHER
CONTINENTAL
PORTS.

HULL

YORK

GOOLE

DONCASTER

SHEFFIELD

LEEDS

BRADFORD

HUDDERSFIELD

DEWSBURY

WAKEFIELD

BARNSLEY

MANCHESTER

OLDHAM

BURY

BOLTON

WIGAN

PRESTON

BLACKPOOL

FLEETWOOD

SOUTHPORT

LIVERPOOL

CHESTER

CROSLEY

MIDLAND ROUTE TO CARLISLE & SCOTLAND

L&NW ROUTE to CARLISLE & SCOTLAND

L&NW ROUTE TO LONDON

MIDLAND ROUTE TO LONDON

TO

LONDONDERRY
BARROW
BELFAST
DOUGLAS

RAMSEY
DOUGLAS
BELFAST
NEWRY
DUNDALK
DROGHEDA
DUBLIN
WEXFORD
WATERFORD
CORK
LLANDUDNO

JOHN A.F. ASPINALL General Manager

LANCASHIRE AND Yorkshire Railway

BRIDLINGTON

FOR
HEALTH
AND
PLEASURE

THE BUSINESS LINE

In his classic work, *Locomotive and Train Working in the Latter Part of the Nineteenth Century*, E. L. Ahrons described the Lancashire & Yorkshire Railway, its locomotives and rolling stock from the early consolidation years of the 1860s and 1870s as 'degenerate' and 'palaeozoic' and this claim was born out by William Barton Wright soon after his appointment as Locomotive Superintendent in 1875 when his survey of the system revealed the decrepit state of the motive power. In his ten years, Barton Wright replaced 95 per cent of the locomotive stock and, without realising it, shook the L&Y directors out of their dividend based outlook into one of efficiency. He paved the way for the complete revolution which was to follow during the years that John A. F. Aspinall (later Sir John), *(see Plate 1)*, would guide the L&Y and make it known as 'The Business Line'.

Aspinall was a fully trained locomotive engineer and was appointed in July 1886 as Chief Mechanical Engineer, but the L&Y Board had no idea that, from that date until his retirement in January 1919, Aspinall would completely revise the entire working of the Company. Starting with locomotives, Aspinall moved on in 1899 to the post of General Manager and began a series of innovations which placed the L&Y in the forefront of railway development in this country through inter-urban electrification, centralised train control and public advertising by extending, throughout the Company, his immense enthusiasm for the business of running a railway. In modern business terminology, Aspinall can be viewed as a great 'manager' as he could build a technically competent and loyal team around him who could, themselves, delegate. Aspinall did not need to display the rigid Victorian authoritarianism of say, Sir Richard Moon. He was always approachable and interested in new ideas but most of all he realised that the public who used the railway, in any capacity whatsoever, met the station staff *(Plate 2)*, not him, and they had to represent the best of the Company. The Company was not just there to provide a service but it had to attract and maintain business.

By 1921, the last full year of independence, the L&Y, as a whole, could hardly be described as 'degenerate', even after the demands of the Great War, and its influence had begun to permeate throughout the entire British railway system as its trainees gained important posts with other railways. It was not the biggest railway in the land nor had it more locomotives than any other but, for its route mileage, it was probably the most intensively worked of all surface lines. It had a tough, no nonsense and workmanlike approach to running a railway, hence the expression 'The Business Line'.

Plate 1 Sir John Audley Frederick Aspinall, (Snowball), then a director of the L&Y and President of the Institution of Civil Engineers, photographed on 26th April 1919.

Author's Collection

◁ In the larger stations, the L&Y provided a tile map of the places it served to help those who were uncertain of the route to take. It was thoughtfully placed between the street and the booking offices. Along with adverts for Bridlington and the Continent are three public telephone boxes, or call offices as they were then termed, of the private National Telephone Company (taken over by the GPO in 1915). The doors between led to the telegraph department, the permanent way department and the district estate office. This picture was taken at Liverpool Exchange in June 1911.

National Railway Museum

? ? BROWNBILL OUTRAM HARRY CARR WINCH ?

NORMAN BARLOW BALL ERNIE CROSSLEY JOHN FLYNN STEAD JOE COATES

TOMMY BELLIS

MANCHESTER VICTORIA : HUB OF THE SYSTEM

Early in their meetings the directors of the L & Y were determined that their Manchester Station was to be the best, not only on the railway itself, nor in Manchester, but, if possible, in the whole country. The latter achievement was far too ambitious but the other two were certainly within those bounds. To further these ends, the directors decided, in late 1843, to name the station after the Queen. It was thought, 'The Victoria Station' was more appropriate than 'The Hunts Bank Station'. No one thought to ask the Royal Personage whether or not she approved and the resolution was just carried out. The full history of the station is detailed elsewhere but it did become the focal point of the entire Lancashire & Yorkshire Railway. Expresses left its 17 platforms for all parts of the system from Liverpool across to Hull and through carriages went to Glasgow, Newcastle, London (several different stations), Birmingham and others. At its zenith the station covered 13½ acres. In 24 hours, 280 trains arrived and 301 departed, whilst 62 passed through non-stop, as did 80 goods trains. Seven trains could have departed simultaneously, although the greatest timetable conjunction was at 5.10p.m. with five trains leaving (3 eastbound, 2 westbound). It was an operator's nightmare, with the east end of the station lying at the bottom of an incline. The LNWR had running powers through it and the Midland Railway had some services which also stopped at Victoria. It was both a terminal and through station and was not really in the centre of the city, or in the city's central business district, yet it had a high percentage of 1st Class and season ticket holders passing through its gates.

Most of the ensuing photographs depict what a traveller using the station about 1914 may have seen had he, or she, the time to look around.

Plate 3 The Hunts Bank approach to the old Victoria Station, about 1870. Of the buildings pictured here, only the original 1844 station now remains, the tall chimneyed building to the left, and that is now partially buried in the 1908 facade. The 1865 booking offices, facing the camera, stand where the present concourse *(Plate 4)* is situated and were demolished only after the building of the present booking complex. The parcel office, more correctly parcel receiving office, with its magnificent destination boards strangely written in several different scripts, opened in January 1861 although the building was constructed in 1847. The parcel office was converted back to offices for the L & Y in about 1894 when the new parcel office near platform 16 was opened. All the offices here were demolished in 1978.

T. Wray Collection

Plate 4 The concourse of Victoria, separating the booking office and waiting rooms from the suburban, terminal platforms. Following completion of the 1905-9 rebuilding and before the Manchester-Bury electrification, these platforms were rigidly organised for specific destinations. The domed building in the background is the restaurant and was built on the site of the 1865 booking offices. Largely because of the time delay system, a method by which the picture was taken on 21st January 1913, there seems to be little activity and the station is exceptionally tidy, although the latter may be for the photographer's benefit. The station seats state plainly 'L.Y.R. VICTORIA'; the traveller being presumed to know that this is the City of Manchester. One of the nearby signboards has the legend 'Reside in the Healthy Northern Suburbs of Manchester'. On discovering this statement, the present writer was left speechless!

National Railway Museum

Plate 6 (below) Until 13th March 1913, Victoria was an open station which necessitated an extra booking office on the island platform 12 & 13. Constructed as part of the 1884 extensions, which brought into use all the through island platforms, the building is typical L&Y design of that period with a dark brown glazed brick base and yellow fireclay bricks above with specially shaped bricks for the window edges, particularly on the upper storey. The mosaic lettering was also a common L&Y practice. Joyce of Whitchurch supplied the clocks throughout the station and the rooms behind these clocks were the station-master's offices. An interesting feature is the pairing of entries and exits to the booking office windows to avoid excessive congestion and multiple queueing at busy times, paired queues being thought better than separate ones. The photograph was taken on 21st January 1913.

National Railway Museum

Plate 5 (above) Having purchased a ticket, the traveller, with time to spare, had several diversions to interest him. One wonder of the station was the overhead parcel carrier. This device was an invention of Aspinall, in 1899, to allow the rapid collection and distribution of parcels to waiting trains across the station. Electrically driven and strictly one-man operated, the skip or basket, holding 15 cwt., could be raised and lowered anywhere and it shuffled backwards and forwards from the main parcel office, next to platform 16, across to platform 1, all day long. At periodic intervals along its path, loading gauges were provided to allow the operator to judge if he would clear the carriage roof which he was crossing. One of these gauges can be seen as a vertical black line in the photograph. The vehicle on the right, with slatted sides, is a four wheel milk truck built, in 1898, to diagram 111 from a reclaimed chassis and was 25 ft. long. The signal-box, known as Victoria Platform Box, is in the background of this view of the island platform 14 & 15.

National Railway Museum

Plate 7 A walk to the west end of platform 12 would probably give a chance to see some engines, such as No. 1110, pictured here, or possibly a Blackpool or Hellifield bound train. In 1909, George Hughes had rebuilt four of Aspinall's 4-4-0s of which No. 1110 was one. The engines received new round top boilers of 180 lb pressure with Schmidt superheaters. The smokeboxes, which were double the size of the previous ones, were finished with the dogged smokebox door and set on a cast steel saddle. Walschaert's valve gear and piston valves were driven by 20 in. cylinders which achieved tremendous hauling power. No. 1110 was later to swap this taper chimney for a parallel one. These rebuilds were so powerful that they worked turn and turn about with the Atlantics. No. 1110 was a Blackpool engine in the charge of Driver J. Worthington and judging from the stock behind the tender, is to work the 4.55 p.m. Manchester Victoria to Blackpool Talbot Road.

The late G. W. Smith

Plate 8 Across from platform 12 was a short refuge siding for an engine waiting to take over a through stopping train. Photographed here is 4-4-2, No. 1424, the last Atlantic built in June 1902. She is in the commonest style for these engines with Hoy safety valve, outside-framed trailing axle, wider chimney and separate handrail on the smokebox door. The date is about 1910. These were the only inside cylinder Atlantics on a British railway system and, despite attempts to oust them, were the top link L&Y motive power until Hughes rebuilt his 4-6-0s. The engine is waiting to work the 4.30 p.m. 40 minute express to Liverpool. No. 1424 was one of the engines fitted with Aspinall's steam drier and the combustion chamber ash hopper can be seen under the boiler barrel.

The late G. W. Smith

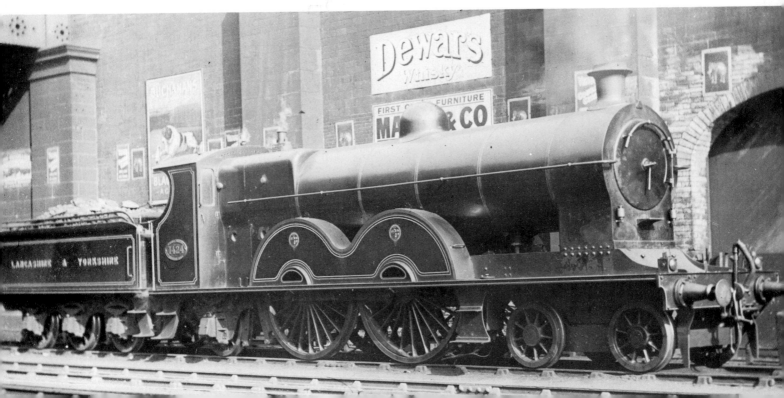

Plate 9

Plates 9 and 10 Two views of the east end of Victoria Station taken about 1895. Plate 9 shows the station throat and gives a full impression of the restricted throat as all major running lines pass in front of the signal box. The gantry controls all movements in and out of the station and, according to a Board of Trade report of 18th September 1896, traffic through this junction was heavier than at any other railway station or junction in England at that time. Plate 10 shows the view from the platforms up towards Miles Platting and the restrictive gradient, encountered immediately on leaving Victoria, can be appreciated. The junction and many of the running lines were drastically altered in the 1903-9 remodelling of the station. Just as period views, these two photographs offer a wealth of detail and the rolling stock, gas lamps, advertising and even the height of the ballast give the clues of 1890s railroading.

National Railway Museum

Plate 10

Plate 11 Aspinall's 2-4-2 tank engines were often to be seen scuttling in and out of the station. Here No. 1045 has been photographed at one of the terminal platforms. This photograph is amongst the last few taken for the L&Y/LNWR on 23rd August 1922 in an attempt to illustrate how Fireman Hartley electrocuted himself whilst attending to the ashpan. Of greater interest are the Hoy safety valves, rarely fitted to 2-4-2 tanks, the rear view of the ground signal and another of Victoria's landmarks, the luggage bridge. This bridge traversed the station, parallel to the subway, and was to facilitate movement of passengers' luggage. Hydraulic lifts, large enough to hold a laden platform trolley and a few people, connected the bridge to each platform. One lift is immediately behind the cab of the engine.

National Railway Museum

Plate 12 This view of a departing Newcastle to Liverpool express, using the North Eastern train of carriages provided for the service, was not seen by the travelling public, as the photographer, George '1400' Smith, is amidst the Deal Street Carriage Sidings. One of Newton Heath's 4-4-0s, No. 344, is attending to its usual station pilot duties as the later series Atlantic heads for Liverpool.

The late G. W. Smith

TRAINS

A selection of pictures showing the types of trains and services provided by the Company.

Plates 13 and 14 Two views of Walkden Troughs on the Pendleton to Hindley line with expresses pictured around 1909. *Plate 13* shows rebuilt 4-4-0, No. 1098, on a Liverpool-Manchester-Leeds/ Bradford train with two of the specially marshalled 'LBL' sets (Liverpool/ Bradford/Leeds). The first set is electrically lit whilst the rear portion was still lit by gas. No. 1098, together with No. 1110 *(Plate 7)*, was rebuilt with Walschaert's valve gear, Schmidt superheater, etc., and is seen still carrying her taper chimney. They were the first engines on the L&Y with Ross 'Pop' safety valves in 1908/9. *Plate 14* is of early Atlantic, No. 1397 with the wide valancing, heading in the opposite direction with a Manchester to Liverpool 'flyer' comprising one elliptical LBL set and a strengthening composite carriage of an earlier style. The L&Y had ten sets of water troughs, which seems excessive for a short haul line, but it was L&Y policy to keep tanks as full as possible to minimise turnaround times on sheds and prevent delays at station stops, all contributing to efficient train running.

J. B. Hodgson Collection

Plate 15 A later series Atlantic on the main line in the Calder Valley. The timbering needed to project the distant signal beyond the goods loop is quite formidable. Two separate sets of carriages make up this express.

S. Sutcliffe Collection

Plate 16 A posed shot of No. 1409 and the modern 1913 rake of mainly 1st Class carriages of the 5.00 p.m. Manchester to Southport businessmen's express. The train is close to Monsall Lane signal-box from where it worked down into Victoria on 5th February 1914.

National Railway Museum

Plate 17 A 2-4-2T locomotive, No. 230, at the head of a long Blackpool bound express at Ansdell. Powerful and economical, these 1911 engines were specifically designed for express work.

A. G. Ellis Collection

Plate 18 No. 1507 passes over Walkden Troughs with the Newcastle to Liverpool express, 2.30 p.m. ex-Victoria, hauling the NER stock used for the service. Some of the plant used in connection with the troughs can be seen. The photograph dates from about 1909.

J. B. Hodgson Collection

Plate 19 Hughes 4-6-0, No. 1506, drifts towards Manchester with a train from Leeds comprising mixed arc and elliptical roofed stock.

The late G. W. Smith

Plate 20 Late in 1920 the first rebuilt 4-6-0, No. 1520, appeared from Horwich Works, a transformed engine, and she simply 'played with her work'. The remainder of the class, barring five, were soon converted and were to be seen at the head of long heavy trains. This view shows No. 1514, the second engine rebuilt, posed for publicity purposes at Southport with 'eleven on' on 20th February 1921.

National Railway Museum

Plate 21 With the amalgamation of the L&Y and LNWR on 1st January 1922, several L&Y engines were tried over former LNWR lines. Amongst the more successful were the Hughes 4-6-0s. Here No. 1653, a new engine of September 1921, built identical to the rebuilds, hurries through Dillicar Troughs with a Preston to Carlisle semi-fast comprised largely of L&Y carriages.

Real Photographs

Plate 22 One of the railmotor services, pictured at Rainford Junction on the service from Ormskirk and which ran into St. Helens after reversal. The service was introduced in July 1906. The Manchester to Liverpool main line runs beneath the bridges. The idea of railmotor services was to reduce costs on branches or compete more effectively with the electric tramcars. In some instances the services were successful and new additional timber halts were provided, but in others they were not. These little trains were often held in great affection by the locals who used them and were a rich source of nicknames, this particular one going under the sobriquet of 'The Chip Train' and 'The Skem Jazzer'.

P. Gibb Collection

Plate 23 A standard Aspinall 0-6-0 is leaving Lockwood and taking the Berry Brow line. The three carriages date from 1894, the centre composite is to diagram 26 and has four 3rd Class and three 1st Class compartments whilst the brakes have five 3rd Class compartments and are to diagram 29. The white centre window on the brake end was reversible to show red, with a red lamp at night. An 0-8-0 locomotive, with only the tender visible, shunts the yard whilst the break van carries a reporting number for a system introduced in August 1915 which ordered the reporting each day, to control at Manchester, of each break van's location. The No. 139 is formed from the van's running number, 13091. The entire scene is typical of the L&Y over the 1917-1922 period.

M. Oates Collection

Plate 24 Local passenger services were generally worked by tank engines with sets of non-corridor carriages. Here 2-4-2T, No. 643 heads a Manchester to Bury train in the days before electrification.

The late G. W. Smith

Plate 25 The L&Y handled prodigious amounts of excursion traffic. Summer Saturdays meant 'Wakes Week' specials to Blackpool or Southport and there were the Whitsun celebrations and the August Bank Holiday trips. In 1899, the booking office at Victoria had to be closed at 5.00 p.m. on Saturday 5th August as there were no carriages left to take the potential customers to their destinations. In fairness, this was largely due to the fact that the LNWR had refused to carry any excursion traffic that day, citing the outbreak of the Boer War as the reason. However, the L&Y did not complain (receipts wise). The L&Y also ran excursions to the Liverpool spring race meeting at Aintree, with the Saturday being Grand National day. For this occasion not only L&Y trains arrived at Aintree (Sefton Arms) and *Plate 25* shows an L&Y train at platform 2, a Liverpool Overhead Railway electric train at platform 3, which has arrived via the Linacre Road spur, and a LNWR train, drawn by an 'Experiment' Class locomotive standing at platform 4, the only day this platform was generally used as the signs, tied to the fences and telegraph posts, show. Aintree Racecourse Station would also be open for the day. This particular scene was photographed on 4th April 1913.

National Railway Museum

Plate 27 The L&Y ran somewhere in the region of 900 goods trains, or merchandise trains, as they were called, per day to a high degree of organization. One feature was the allowing of the faster classes of merchandise the 'Right Away', Class R and 'Special Express Merchandise' (Class A) trains, usually hauling perishable goods, to run in front of, or pass, stopping passenger trains. One such train, a Class A, is shown in *Plate 27*. It is a fish special with 11 vans to diagram 72, all with oil axleboxes, dual fitted and piped with a converted six wheel brake for the guard. The engine is Atlantic, No. 1395. This must have been one of the L&Y's most colourful trains as the engine was black, lined in red and white and the fish vans, when clean, were a very pale green and the guard's brake was in 'passenger' tan and lake. This photograph, taken on 23rd June 1913, is a posed shot as the selfsame configuration of vans is headed by 0-6-0, No. 1253 in another picture taken on the same day.

National Railway Museum

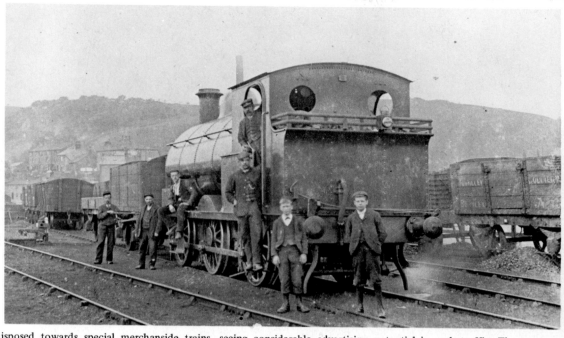

Plate 28 Short trip working and yard shunting were generally in the hands of 0-6-0 tanks, the vast majority being Aspinall's saddle tank conversion of the standard Barton Wright 0-6-0. The scene is Todmorden coal-yard and, judging by the types of goods wagons visible, this is a turn of the century view.

J. B. Hodgson Collection

Plate 29 The L&Y was well disposed towards special merchanside trains, seeing considerable advertising potential in such traffic. The Accrington firm of billiard table makers, E. J. Riley & Company, used these special trains on several occasions. They were often made up of four or six wheel passenger brake vans converted for parcels or perishable traffic to be consigned by passenger trains *(see Plates 163/4)*. In this case, rebuilt 4-4-0, No. 1221 heads a train of 12 six wheelers with a completed order for London. The train is approaching Accrington West cabin and is signalled for the Burnley line. With considerable humour, the photographer has, on 14th May 1914, lined up the train beside one of Riley's large advertising hoardings which could be seen on the approach to Accrington.

National Railway Museum

THE MIDDLE YEARS

The L&Y fared worse than most railways with their locomotive development in the middle period from 1850 to 1875. A succession of inadequate designs, under-powered engines and hopelessly weak locomotive management, which led to an indescribably bad train service, gave the Company a fearful reputation with the public. The engines were just not powerful enough, they could not adequately complete their work and there was little ingenuity, foresight or innovation about their design and construction. It is a fair indictment to say, of the locomotive strength on the line at that time that the best engines were those the L&Y had purchased new from the LNWR.

Plate 30 (above) *Diomed* was the East Lancashire Railway's locomotive, No. 10, but this particular engine was a Jenkins 2-2-2, built in 1849 for the Manchester & Leeds Railway, the design having been considerably influenced by Sir John Hawkshaw. Originally M&L, No. 131, she became L&Y No. 90, and in 1862 her number was swapped for the name and number of an East Lancashire engine. Although the amalgamation of the L&Y and the ELR took place in 1859, the two parts were operated more or less as separate companies until the middle 1870s. *Diomed* was rebuilt as a 2-4-0 in 1866 and disposed of in 1869, never returning to L&Y stock. The photograph, like all the ones on this page, was taken at Manchester Road in Burnley, the former M&L terminus, and the engine's usual duty was the working of passenger trains from the East Lancashire lines in Burnley to Todmorden, and this might well have been the reason for the transfer.

J. B. Hodgson Collection

Plates 31 (below) and 32 (right) The standard L&Y goods engine of the 1860s was the 0-4-2 type built to Jenkins' design but again with Hawkshaw's influence. *Plate 31* shows a rare quarter-front view of No. 140, a locomotive built in April 1854. The class had 15 in. x 24 in. cylinders and 4 ft. 9 in. coupled wheels. There were 33 engines and they were painted green. No. 140 was replaced in January 1880 without being rebuilt, retaining the raised firebox with copper dome originally designed for coke burning, although it would have become a coal burner in the late 1860s. The engines which were rebuilt were painted black. *Plate 32* shows the cab view of an 0-4-2, probably taken from the roof of a carriage, and is absolutely fascinating. The spectacle plates were later replaced by weather-boards; meanwhile the footplate crews were incredibly exposed.

B. C. Lane Collection and Author's Collection

As with many railways, photography caught up with developments from about 1870 onwards. The early pieces had largely gone or had been rebuilt but there was the sorry parade of Hurst, Jenkins and Yates engines for the photographers to capture. However, change was on the horizon, and even the early pictures of Barton Wright's engines display a stronger, more workman-like approach to getting on with the job.

Plates 33 and 34 Holme and Stuart are Jenkins 2-4-0s of the same class. In Plate 33, Holme portrays the original 1860s appearance of these engines with weatherboard and four wheel tender. The greatest problem is that there is no surviving record of a L&Y engine being named Holme and yet here it is. Some authors have suggested that this may be engine No. 335, the one built following the eleven named after L&Y directors, but there has been no positive proof or denial of this fact to date. Plate 34 shows Stuart with the later look of these engines with a new Yates cab, plus number plate which only came to be fitted to L&Y engines after 1878. It is also fitted with a six wheel tender. No. 288 was further rebuilt in June 1886 to look like No. 336 (Plate 62).

B. C. Lane Collection and J. B. Hodgson Collection

Plate 35 The standard Jenkins 0-6-0 goods engine looked like No. 668 Bucephalus, shown here. This engine was built in March 1860 with 4 ft. 10 in. coupled wheels and 15 in. x 24 in. cylinders. Although built by the L&Y at Miles Platting, the engine was drafted on to the East Lancashire section, thus acquiring her name. She is pictured in the form following her July 1874 rebuilding and was withdrawn in July 1881. From March 1875, former East Lancashire section engines received number plates of the style later to be expanded throughout the L&Y system until 1923 (see number-plate in Plate 276). At this time, about 1875, goods trains were often termed 'Luggage Trains'.

B. C. Lane Collection

Plate 36 East Lancashire Railway locomotive No. 36 *Milo*, a Sharp Stewart 2-4-0 (Works No. 575) of June 1849. The engine appears to be as built except, possibly, for the weatherboard. A gorgeous Victorian locomotive with smokebox wing plates, huge brass numbers, a massive dome with safety-valves and outside framing. When rebuilt with a proper cab and plain dome boiler, Ahrons reckoned that this type was the fastest and smartest on the L & Y. *Milo* was rebuilt in 1863 and lasted until June 1878. The location is thought to be Colne and the five compartment carriage is also probably East Lancashire.

B. C. Lane Collection

Plate 37 The engine is No. 93, formerly M & L No. 133, which started life as a Jenkins 2-2-2 *(see Plate 30)*. In November 1872 she was rebuilt as a 2-4-0 acquiring a new boiler and firebox with Naylor safety-valves and a Yates cab although still managing to look very frail. No. 93 was withdrawn in August 1879.

J. B. Hodgson Collection

te 38 Caledonia Street, Bradford,
ound 1875, and an excellent view of
d-1870s railroading. The engine is No.
8, a Yates 4 ft. 0 in. saddle tank of
ril 1871. The drum-like object on the
otplate is a sandbox and in front of
is is the familiar jack carried by most
er L & Y engines, although this is just
out the earliest view of one. This
gine lasted until October 1894. The
cture contains many items of interest
the sidelines including gas lamps, the
msy level crossing gate, crossing
per's bothy and the signal with
parated arm and spectacle plate. The
ossing was on the incline out of
change Station near the original
gine shed with the approach roads
ing in the foreground which must
ve been difficult to work, even in
ose days. Pedestrians have already
en segregated on to the bridge in
eparation for the closure of the
ossing.

J. B. Hodgson Collection

Plate 39 Another Miles Platting built engine drafted on to the East Lancashire lines and thus acquiring the name of her forebears. No. 637 was built as a well tank in November 1873 to a Yates design. She was rebuilt as a saddle tank in June 1877 and withdrawn in November 1889. Although diminutive, these were sturdy engines but the addition of a saddle tank, especially when full of water, gave these engines the extra adhesive weight they required and they were latterly regarded as quite powerful. Although working on the East Lancashire lines, the engine is in L & Y green with white and black lining.

B. C. Lane Collection

Plates 42 (top right) and 43 (middle right) No. 703 *Emperor* pictured before and after rebuilding. *Plate 42* shows a standard Yates 5 ft. 0 in. 0-6-0 built in January 1870 with bent over weatherboard. During Barton Wright's days it received a dome boiler, a new standard cab and the clearing up of the external pipework. *Plate 43* shows a much more modern looking engine but it received no brakes other than those on the tender. This fact, coupled with the massive numbers of Barton Wright 0-6-0s and the incoming Aspinall 0-6-0s, resulted in the engine soon becoming obsolete and she was withdrawn in August 1898. Of particular interest in *Plate 43* is the bracket signal with the single spectacle glass to the arms as, at this point in time, the light for 'all clear' was still white. Standard Railway Signalling Company parts have been supplied which has resulted in the use of one L & Y and one Great Central type finial!

J. B. Hodgson Collection

Plate 44 (bottom right) Another Yates 5 ft. 0 in. 0-6-0, but *Samson* was refitted at Bury works, hence the slightly different style of cab. No. 612 was built at Miles Platting in December 1870 and went to work on the East Lancashire lines. The name was removed in the late 1880s and she was withdrawn in June 1903.

J. B. Hodgson Collection

Plate 40 Yates' standard 2-4-0 express engine, although the number is unknown. At this time, L & Y engines had their number only on the buffer beam and this is one of the later half-dozen rounded rear splasher engines of 1872/3. There is a combined pony wheel splasher and sandbox and these engines were amongst the first fitted with the Naylor safety-valve. These engines ran for about 20 years until being withdrawn in 1893/4.

J. B. Hodgson Collection

Plate 41 A little later in 1873, the former East Lancashire Railway works at Bury turned out four new engines of Yates express 2-4-0 type, but with their own detail differences such as raised footplating, domed boilers, ELR brass capped chimneys and with the Naylor safety-valves fitted transversely. In later years a different style of Yates cab was fitted. The engines replaced ex-East Lancashire stock and took their names and L & Y numbers, although *Reindeer* shown here is still in ELR dark green livery with red and white lining and hand painted number; the frames were red brown. The engine was placed in service in November 1873 and withdrawn during 1893.

B. C. Lane Collection

Plate 45   No. 189 was a Yates 4ft. 0in. 0-6-0 saddle tank built in September 1875 with 15in. cylinders which were later enlarged to 16in. No. 189 was part of a class dating back to 1868 which also included No. 158 *(Plate 38)*. It is probable that she was built with the cab in view and the chimney (alas photographically distorted) is the Yates original. She is shown here in the green L&Y livery and the lining out of white and black is extremely complex, including under the saddle tank, the curve of the bunker, sandbox and buffer beams which are also gently curved. The locomotive lamps and brackets are also interesting. She was withdrawn in September 1893.

J. B. Hodgson Collection

Plate 46   A Yates 2-4-0, No. 4, the first one built in October 1870, passing Shoe Mill, Baxenden on the bank out of Accrington. Judging from the clarity of the original print, the engine has stopped at the signal and is about to restart. The contemporary L&Y ballast arrangement of sleeper ends protruding out of the ash can be seen. No. 4 was withdrawn in June 1896.

A. Wilkinson Collection

Plate 47   A carriage from the middle years is this old full brake of the 1860s. No. 181 was built under Fay with a most interesting slab-sided construction with broad waist panelling and half round beading. This particular piece, 24ft. 6in. long, 6ft. 9in. wide and 10ft. 10in. high, had survived as a Travelling Van with the Low Moor breakdown train and on such duties these carriages lasted well into LMS days. It affords an insight into the discomforts of mid-Victorian rail travel.

B. C. Lane Collection

Plate 48 Berry Brow Station on the enistone line with a relatively new Barton right 0-6-0, No. 859, shunting. This was e station where engines were carved into e rock face behind the down platform, here the shelter is, and which the station-aster is facing. No. 859 spent 14 years a tender locomotive being rebuilt as a ddle tank in January 1899 eventually eing withdrawn as British Railways comotive No. 51504 in August 1956.

J. B. Hodgson Collection

Plate 49 Holme Station on the Todmorden to Burnley line around 1893. The engine, No. 47, was a Yates 2-4-0 to be withdrawn in 1894. Since its construction in 1871, the engine has acquired a Yates cab, a dome and a Barton Wright chimney and there is a good opportunity to view the clumsy looking Yates smokebox door hinge. The carriages are a typical set of five from the 1870s now relegated to branch line work, with four Attock four wheelers and a Fay design brake with the characteristic birdcage end. The signal behind the train carries arms for both lines, whilst the point rodding rests on its own timber stools. The train has come from Todmorden. *(See also Plate 89).*

R. Stansfield Collection

Plate 50 Eastwood Station on the Manchester to Leeds line in the 1880s. The station was in one of the narrowest parts of the valley and was perched half way up the north side whilst the turnpike ran below, on the valley floor. Both the platforms and goods facilities were staggered either side of the level crossing with the station house and offices set into the cutting. The land for the station was given to the M & L by Mr Eastwood in 1842, although the station had been opened on 1st March 1841. The signal cabin, a Saxby & Farmer type, lasted into the 1970s. The station was used by one of the L & Y directors for whom a morning train from Leeds was stopped especially to allow him to get to Manchester for board meetings.

J. B. Hodgson Collection

Plate 51 Heckmondwike on the Spen Valley line around 1875. From here to Liversedge the line was laid single track. The platform canopy, supports and low wooden platform were later to be swept away, displaying the offices behind, when the station was moved to a new location in 1886. Another view of the old wooden yard cranes can be seen in *Plate 30*. Here too, are the early L & Y telegraph poles with long and short arms alternately placed.

B. C. Lane Collection

THE COMING OF
BARTON WRIGHT

Plate 52 Very soon after his appointment, Barton Wright had to acquire new engines quickly and he negotiated for, and obtained, eight 0-4-2 engines of Great Northern design 'off the peg' from Sharp Stewart which were originally destined for the GN. As part of the deal, the GNR order was completed later by Sharp Stewart. Seen here, in green, is the first one delivered, No. 605 which replaced the ex-East Lancashire rebuilt 0-6-0 *Cyclops*, but under the Barton Wright regime the names were not perpetuated. Built in March 1876 as Sharp Stewart Works No. 2576, No. 605 was eventually withdrawn in May 1901. On the GN this type of locomotive was for secondary duties but such was the paucity of strong motive power at the time that these engines were the most powerful on the L&Y and they spent most of their early life on expresses, eventually becoming one of the most useful class of engines on the system. One or two engines received the lined out black livery and cabside crest. The double head-lamps show the old express passenger code.

J. B. Hodgson Collection

Plates 53 and 54 L&Y goods motive power was also in such a poor state, and the Company workshops so disorganized, that Barton Wright was forced to carry on the policy that he had adopted at the Madras Railway, of buying what amounted to standard builders' types, if he was to get the L&Y back to fulfilling a decent service, using adequate locomotives, as quickly as possible. *Plate 53* shows NO. 529, the second engine supplied by Kitson late in July 1876 with the stovepipe chimney and different cab fitted to the first two engines. Apart from the rear box splasher it was identical to some Taff Vale Railway engines but Barton Wright's judgement was sound, as these engines were to prove far stronger than anything else that had previously worked on the L&Y. *Plate 54* shows No. 565, one of the second batch ordered from Sharp Stewart, although all were delivered before the Kitson order was complete. No. 565 was put into service in October 1877 and converted, in April 1891, to a saddle tank by Aspinall, one of the earliest so completed. Barton Wright's new green livery with two white and one black line is shown in this view. As ever, the proud crew pose for their photograph to be taken, but on this occasion, there were two cleaners with their cotton waste cleaning bundles as well.

J. B. Hodgson Collection and B. C. Lane Collection

BARTON WRIGHT AND ASPINALL ENGINES

When Barton Wright commenced work for the L&Y, his first task was to tour the system and assess the position thoroughly. From this, he took three major decisions which had fundamental influences on the L&Y for the rest of its life. Firstly, the Railway must be re-equipped, not just with engines that could cope, but with engines that would be masters at their job for years to come. Secondly, the new engine types should be standardized across the system, meaning not only the same types in Liverpool and Goole but also that engine parts appertaining to different types should be interchangeable. Thirdly, there was to be an improvement in maintenance, not just in overhauling locomotives but also in looking after them whilst out on the road. To an economist these decisions were wise as it meant greater loads hauled by engines, quick cheap turnaround times and more efficient running of engines. In the long run this led to a reduction in costs per mile per engine.

The first of Barton Wright's practical decisions was to drastically reduce the building of new locomotives at the Miles Platting Works and to purchase from outside contractors, thus releasing the works to over-haul and rebuild engines. Close consultation with the engine builders, especially Kitson's, resulted in four new engine classes, basically one for each type of work, fast passenger, local passenger, goods and general work including shunting and in ten years some five hundred and ten engines, two hundred and eighty 0-6-0s, seventy two 0-4-4Ts, ninety four 4-4-0s and sixty four 0-6-2Ts, were supplied to the L&Y. Embodied in these four classes was the concept of standardization of parts, for all had the same cylinders, valves and, despite minor internal differences, boilers, and all were fully interchangeable. To look after this stock Barton Wright soon realized that Miles Platting could never cope and the hunt began for a site for a new works, culminating at Horwich in 1884, and it was Barton Wright who was largely responsible for the layout of the new works. He also found time to design a standard engine shed for erection as a new or replacement building. Many structures housing locomotives were the original 'temporary' buildings sorely in need of replacement and a large percentage of locomotives could not be accommodated under cover. From 1885, the saw-tooth roof and bay windowed shedmaster's office type of building began to appear all over the system.

To a certain extent Aspinall was fortunate to inherit the work of Barton Wright. The locomotive stock was newer and in better order and the new works was within sight of completion. He could have sat back and rested on Barton Wright's laurels but to his eternal credit he did not. Aspinall adopted the Barton Wright principles; standardization, engines to be masters of their job for years to come and high standards of maintenance. He began his own series of locomotive classes, engines which were to be the epitome of efficiency, high density traffic working and load shifting. From the reign of both it was to mean the sudden demise of many underpowered engines, often after relatively short working lives, but efficiency and standardization were the keywords of the revolution.

Plate 56 (below) For express work Barton Wright designed a 4-4-0, the first of this wheel arrangement on the L&Y. The first engine came from Sharp Stewart in August 1880 but No. 653 was Works No. 2917, the last of the initial order of eight engines supplied with the four wheel tender. In this particular picture, the engine has been painted in Barton Wright's green passenger livery, lined in chrome yellow and dark green for the Stephenson Centenary at Newcastle in 1881. This engine was the first to receive the newly devised crest and the gold tender monogram 'L&YR', shaded red. On later engines, the crest was moved higher up the cabside. On the cab roof is a small bracket to carry the communication cord to the second whistle. Also visible is the coloured background to the number plate, indigo in this case for Sharp Stewart.

B. C. Lane Collection

Plate 55 (above) Having provided an adequate goods engine, Barton Wright turned his attention to passenger traffic, beginning with 0-4-4Ts for local work. These engines were far superior to any other locomotive already working similar trains on the L&Y. Four companies built the engines but No. 2, shown here, was a Sharp Stewart engine (Works No. 3309) built in November 1885 and given the number 916. She was renumbered in 1886 and withdrawn, by Hughes, in March 1910. Several engines of this type were drafted on to carriage warming duties after modifications.

A. G. Ellis Collection

Plate 57 This photograph shows No. 865, formerly named *Prince of Wales*, at Poulton. Modifications over the years have included Aspinall-type chimney, altered steps, replacement whistle, removal of nameplate, black passenger livery and different tender. Like many of her sister locomotives, this 4-4-0 had a relatively short life of 20 years, being withdrawn in June 1905. The demise of these locomotives was caused by increased loads and more powerful locomotives coming on to the scene.

The late J. M. Tomlinson

Plate 58 Barton Wright originated the 0-6-2T type in this country by rebuilding a Jenkins 0-6-0 goods engine (Plate 35) starting with No. 333 in 1879. Based on this experience and in conjunction with Kitsons, Barton Wright had ten new engines built, starting in 1880, with 4 ft. 6 in. wheels. In April 1881, the wheel size was increased to 5 ft. 1 in. and supply was recommenced with fourteen more Kitson engines. Shown here is No. 223, a Dubs engine, (Works No. 1664) of January 1883. Originally No. 185, she was renumbered for accounting purposes and was withdrawn in November 1910 without being reboiled. This photograph shows the engine with a cast chimney, green livery and a number-plate dated 1882. The clock tower over the time office in the background was a feature of Agecroft shed and appears in many photographs of this era.

J. B. Hodgson Collection

Plate 59 Two more 0-6-2Ts with black passenger livery and different lettering. No. 655, (Dubs Works No. 1638 of September 1882 and formerly No. 640), closest to the camera, is in the Hughes style, whilst further away, No. 688, (Dubs Works No. 1643 of November 1882) is in the Hoy style. Both engines lasted well into LMS days being withdrawn as No. 11609, in March 1928, and 11612 in October 1932 respectively. The photograph was taken at Newton Heath shed and No. 655 is allocated to shed No. 1, Newton Heath.

J. B. Hodgson Collection

Plate 60 Another photograph of a Barton Wright 0-6-0 which completes the successful quartet which he introduced. No. 773 (Beyer Peacock No. 2013 of February 1882), shows the more unusual appearance of these engines with six wheel tenders fitted with weatherboards. She is in Barton Wright's later green livery and was converted to a saddle tank in 1895.

J. B. Hodgson Collection

BARTON WRIGHT CONVERSIONS

Plate 61 Whilst private locomotive building firms were creating new products for the L & Y, Barton Wright was using the Miles Platting Works for repair and conversion of the existing locomotive stock. Besides reboilering and refurbishing, *(Plates 62 and 63)*, some major conversions were undertaken. The main 'target' class of engines was the Jenkins 4 ft. 10 in. 0-6-0s *(Plate 35)* and out of the 0-6-0s came 0-4-4Ts, 0-6-2Ts and the 0-6-0 saddle tanks, as No. 690 shown here. This engine had started life as a Jenkins 0-6-0 in May 1867 and had been drafted on to the East Lancashire section with the name *Sisyphus*. In October 1884 she was rebuilt as a 0-6-0ST with 4 ft. 0 in. wheels and lost her name at the same time. The cab was not of the standard style and the engine had also acquired a new Barton Wright chimney, Ramsbottom safety-valves, combined sandbox and front splasher and the black livery with two red bands of lining used on goods engines. The number-plate has been altered to 1884, the year of conversion. The engine was withdrawn in March 1898. It appears that there may be a hint of saddle tanks to come *(see Plate 87)* in this design.

J. B. Hodgson Collection

Plate 62 Not all of Barton Wright's rebuilds were as drastic as No. 690, as he was content just to reboiler the stronger engines. No. 336 was a Jenkins 2-4-0 of March 1865, the same class as No. 288 *Stuart (Plate 34)*. Comparison between the photographs will show that a new firebox, boiler and chimney have all been substituted. The work was carried out in November 1877 and the engine ran until April 1893.

B. C. Lane Collection

Plate 63 No. 103 is a Yates 2-4-0, built ten years later than No. 336, in March 1875. This engine was the only one built with 5 ft. 6 in. wheels and intended for fast goods work. She was alleged to have been built with a dome but photographic evidence has disproved this, the dome probably being acquired in Barton Wright days. Among other items altered, the engine has managed to obtain a Horwich chimney, vacuum brake and black passenger livery, whilst the Naylor safety-valves were soon to be phased out of L&Y use. She was amongst the last of the Yates 2-4-0 type to be withdrawn, in May 1899.

J. B. Hodgson Collection

Plates 64 and 65 Despite the ordering and rebuilding policies of Barton Wright, such had been the increase in traffic that when Aspinall became Chief Mechanical Engineer there was still a shortage of engines. One of the types chosen to be built was the 4-4-0 but this time Beyer Peacock was to build thirty with a few of Aspinall's modifications which included raising the boiler centre line, smaller bogie wheels. Joy valve gear with external reversing rod and fluted coupling rods. Beneath it all they were really a continuation of the Barton Wright class. All were built between July 1888 and April 1889. *Plate 64* is a later view of No. 1005, photographed at Poulton, showing the full passenger livery and lettering. *Plate 65* shows a three quarter rear view of No. 999 and includes some of the cab, the shed plate and a chance to study the gold block 'L&Y' inscription introduced in 1891. No. 999 was later rebuilt by Hughes with a Belpaire boiler and survived until 1932. At the time both photographs were taken, Nos. 999 and 1005 were attached to No. 30 shed, Fleetwood. No. 1005 lasted, unaltered, until December 1931.

J. B. Hodgson Collection and
B. C. Lane Collection

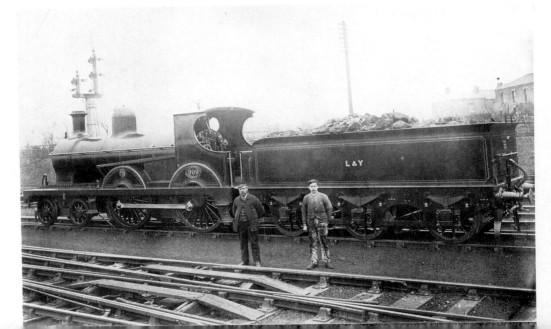

Plates 66 to 68 With Horwich Works nearing completion, the time had come for the first locomotives to be put in hand there. The express passenger fleet was being augmented and Aspinall turned to suburban passenger locomotives and designed a new engine for this job. The experiences from Barton Wright's 0-4-4T design were incorporated in the new locomotive. The same size coupled driving wheels were used, but placed centrally to obtain a better balance, and radial axleboxes for the carrying wheels were chosen in place of a bogie. The boiler from the new 4-4-0s was slightly modified and used in the design, and water and coal capacities were increased. Thus a completely new, but logically improved, design was the first lot built at the new works. *Plate 66* shows No. 301 of October 1892 (Works No. 184) pictured as she ran for the first ten years of her life with no Company identification other than crest and number-plate. The engine type also established the black livery lined out white and red. From the first locomotive built, the wording on the number-plates was changed to read 'L&YRy Co. Makers'. No. 301, a 2-4-2T, is pictured at Southport and one of the old single spectacle signals is in the right background. *Plate 67* shows a 2-4-2T on a Manchester to Blackburn train passing the LNWR Exchange Station. After nearly ten years and 210 locomotives, Aspinall changed the design by extending the rear frames thus allowing for extra coal and water capacity. In this way he hoped to extend the range of these engines. Sixty were built, many of which were subsequently rebuilt with Belpaire boilers and superheaters. *Plate 68* shows No. 346, (built 5th December 1898), at Blackpool Central shed in the Hughes unlettered style of livery adopted in 1922 when the L&Y had merged with the LNWR. No. 346 remained unaltered until withdrawn in 1939 as LMS No. 10833.   *J. B. Hodgson Collection*

Plates 69 to 71   Like his predecessor, Aspinall's next priority was for goods traffic and to satisfy the demands of the traffic department, an improved 0-6-0 was designed. The boiler from the 4-4-0s and 2-4-2Ts was slightly modified again and the wheels increased to 5 ft. 1 in. which made the locomotives better suited for passenger work. However, it was the increased pressure and heating surfaces of the boiler which were their major improving features. *Plate 69* shows No. 341, (Works No. 245 of 23rd August 1893), at Agecroft and the locomotive is very much as built with the 1879 black livery and double red lining, having the gold L Y R monogram of the same period on the tender. Aspinall's flush smokebox door can be seen as can the sockets for the lamps, (as per L N W R), before lampirons were standardized. *Plate 70* is a cab view of this rugged but simple engine type. A docket for the shed plate is attached to the cab roof. *Plate 71* is a later view of the class in full passenger livery. No. 214 (Works No. 379 of 1st July 1895) was photographed in May 1914 at Bolton shed (No. 14) her home depot, as part of a series of photographs to instruct and educate enginemen. Standard 20 ton Locomotive Coal wagons stand near the coaling stage. Of the two engines, No. 341 lasted the longer being withdrawn as B R No. 52216 in December 1958.

J. B. Hodgson Collection and National Railway Museum

Plates 72 to 75 Aspinall never intended the Beyer Peacock 4-4-0s to be anything other than a stopgap. Train loads were still rising, traffic increasing and an even more powerful express engine was needed. The result was his own design of 4-4-0, with massive 7 ft. 3 in. driving wheels encompassing experiences from Ireland. The first engine was outshopped in March 1891 and from the start these locomotives were masters of their work. *Plate 72* shows No. 1108 from the first batch (Lot 7). The location and date are unknown but the engine has swapped her original Barton Wright tender for a new Aspinall one with the newer style of block letters 'L&Y' on the tender. The picture also affords the chance to see L&Y track and ballasting comprising rail and sleepers on a chipping base with ash cover filling the gaps. *Plate 73* is an earlier view of a later engine. No. 1226, from the 1894 batch, has the old socket headlamps and must be very much as built. The driving wheel brake-blocks are very worn which suggests heavy use. *Plate 74* is a picture from 1898 when No. 318 was loaned to the GNR for testing against GN 4-4-0, No. 1310. Especially for his friend Aspinall, H. A. Ivatt had, for this engine, a tender painted black and lined and lettered. The tender was necessary as the GN had no water troughs at that time and the L&Y tenders had insufficient water capacity, and this created an interesting combination. *Plate 75* shows No. 1099 near Middleton Junction with a Manchester to York train, close to the end of the L&Y period as a Hughes power class plate is high up on the cab side. The leading carriage is one of ten built with extra parcel capacity for through trains to the NER. Two vans were attached to each train and a L&Y guard was in each van in charge of the separate L&Y and NER parcels at opposite ends of the train. The vans were assigned to Diagram 52.

J. B. Hodgson Collection, B. C. Lane Collection and the late G. W. Smith

Plate 75

Plates 76 and 77 Aspinall's next design, in 1891, was the famous 0-4-0 saddle tank for shunting in docks and restricted goods yards. The basis of the type was a Vulcan design, which Aspinall enlarged slightly, resulting in larger cabs and increasing the water capacity by extending the saddle tank over the smokebox. These diminutive engines with 3 ft. 0 in. driving wheels were extremely useful and many lasted into the 1960s with others being sold out of service to works and quarries. *Plate 76* shows one of the first Aspinall engines, No. 310, with the board against the cab side sheets to keep out the weather and the 'coffee pot' spark arrester used around Liverpool Docks. *Plate 77* shows two of the Hughes-built engines Nos. 19 and 2 (both built in 1910). No. 19 has the Hughes class plate (Class 21) and the disc spark arrester for use in and around warehouses. No. 2 was withdrawn in 1931 but No. 19 is preserved and is currently on the Keighley & Worth Valley Railway.

J. B. Hodgson Collection and
B. C. Lane Collection

Plate 78

Plate 79

Plates 78 to 81 Aspinall was just beaten into bringing out the first British 4-4-2 by his longtime friend, Harry Ivatt of the Great Northern Railway, but when Aspinall's engine was put into service it was, without doubt, the most dramatic and impressive locomotive yet seen upon a British railway. The huge driving wheels and high pitched boiler seemed to exude power and North Eastern Railway locomen gave them the nickname 'Zulu Chiefs' as they were tall, black and powerful. Destined to be the only British inside cylinder Atlantics, these engines were at the head of L&Y expresses for over 20 years and only Hughes-rebuilt 4-6-0s ousted them from the top link jobs. Much has been written about these engines and these photographs show some of their stages of development and their external appearance. *Plate 78* shows No. 1395 of 24th April 1899, very much as first turned out with Ramsbottom safety-valves, fluted coupling rods, low cut cab side sheets, continuous style handrails and double lamp irons below the narrow chimney. These engines gained a new tender of a wider style with coal rails. *Plate 79* shows No. 702 around 1904 at a very interesting stage of development. The engine has acquired the Hoy safety-valve and has been converted to piston valves, the blimp below the smokebox door. New lubricators have been fitted and the lower handrail removed, but the major alteration had taken place in March 1903 when the engine received a Davies & Metcalfe exhaust steam injector, (the pipework outside the rear carrying wheel), as an experiment. This photograph was taken at York with a Great Eastern 4-2-2 behind the Atlantic's tender. No. 702 was destined to be badly damaged in an accident at Ormskirk in 1910 resulting in the locomotive requiring considerable repair and alteration to the main frames. *Plate 80* shows an Atlantic at work, No. 737 on a Manchester to York express at Middleton in the early 1920s. The engine is in roughly the same condition as No. 1406 shown in *Plate 81*, the second engine of the second series, turned out on 3rd February 1902. No. 1406 has received many of the alterations made over the years with the new Hughes early style smokebox door, split handrails, wide chimney, flat coupling rods, new firebox with three washout plugs per side, Hoy 'dummy tit' safety-valve and outside axleboxes to the trailing axle, (a 1905 development). The narrow valancing of the second series gave a more balanced look to the engine. One peculiar feature is the paint finish. The Hughes class plate is visible but, apart from the number-plate, there is no Company identification whatsoever. The period is 1922 before the LNW Division 'B' livery was settled, hence no tender legend and no Company crests appear. For the final developments of this class see *Plate 131*.

J. B. Hodgson Collection, the late G. W. Smith and the late W. H. Whitworth

Plates 82 and 83 Two years before the Atlantics came on to the scene, in 1897, Aspinall had designed an 0-6-0 side tank type. They were termed 'Rapid' shunters but the reason for their introduction has never been made particularly clear. The conversions, from Barton Wright's 0-6-0s, were proceeding apace (see Plate 87) and the work done by those engines was well up to standard, therefore these new shunters hardly seemed necessary. Although called 'Rapid' shunters, locomen regarded them as anything but, as the regulators left much to be desired. They preferred the saddle tanks. However, LNW crews thought them superior to anything available when they received a few of these locomotives after 1922.

Plate 82 (above) shows No. 1354 as first built with spring buffers, Richardson valves, Belpaire firebox (one of the earliest applications in this country), and double lamp brackets below the chimney. She is in the black goods livery with the double red lining and displays the very short wheelbase which was a feature of these engines. No. 1354 was withdrawn in December 1914 after a working life of only seventeen years.
Plate 83 (right) shows No. 505, a little later in life, with wooden block buffers, altered slide bars, spark arrester and Hoy livery. The picture is at Sandhills shed (No. 18), about 1918, and includes the shed cat.

Author's Collection and the late E. Mason

Plates 84 (above) and 85 (top right) Although the 0-8-0s were not introduced until April 1900, a little after Aspinall had become General Manager, they were really to his engine design and were the answer to the traffic department's request for a powerful coal train shifter. Two rather unconventional views of the class are shown here. Plate 84 shows No. 676, one of the first twenty engines built, and whose boiler blew up on 11th March 1901, approximately two miles from Knottingley, whilst working a coal train, killing both driver and fireman. It was subsequently found that the bronze stays, with which the firebox was held, whilst strong enough to do the job themselves, did not stay 'tight' and leakage past them increased over a period of time causing the failure. The photograph shows the initial appearance of these engines with the Atlantic-type six wheel tender and narrow chimney. Whether this photograph was taken before or after the explosion is not known. Plate 85 shows engine No. 710 with a wide stovepipe chimney on 14th December 1910 before undergoing some draughting experiments. Little else has changed except that the new standard eight wheel tender has been paired with the engine. This is a good illustration of the Aspinall flush smokebox door with the two extra dogs at the bottom to prevent excessive warping. Still on view are the cab front doors some eight years after the order has gone out for their removal and the locomotive is photographed at Horwich Works.

J. B. Hodgson Collection and National Railway Museum

Plate 86 (below) Like his predecessor, Aspinall rebuilt and converted older engines to get the maximum life from them. This photograph shows engine No. 659, one of the Sharp Stewart GNR type 0-4-2s, brought in by Barton Wright in 1876. Aspinall had all eight of these locomotives reboilered around 1894/5. New chimneys, domes and Ramsbottom safety-valves were fitted in addition to the closing in of the splashers. Complete with the full black passenger livery, the external appearance of these engines altered considerably. Photographed at Leeds, No. 659 was withdrawn in July 1900 and should be compared with *Plate 52*.

B. C. Lane Collection

Plate 87 (below) Aspinall's most famous rebuilding achievement was carried out on Barton Wright's 0-6-0 goods tender engines. The conversion to tank engines was actually quite simple and fairly cheap, and a very reliable and easily handled engine resulted. Conversion began in 1891 with No. 543 as Aspinall's more powerful 0-6-0 goods engines were becoming more plentiful. The method was to fit a saddle tank over the boiler, lengthen the rear main frames a little, fit a new overall cab and bunker and then return the locomotive to traffic. It took until 1900 to convert all barring the last fifty Barton Wright 0-6-0s, although there were also plans to rebuild these. Some engines ran as little as twelve or thirteen years with tenders but for sixty or more years as saddle tanks. No. 558, shown here with very worn brake shoes and painted in goods black livery with red lining, was built in August 1877 by Sharp Stewart, converted in July 1891, became LMS No. 11304 and was withdrawn in December 1961. Her sister engine, LMS No. 11305, another Horwich Works shunter and formerly No. 553, was the last operative L&Y engine on BR, being withdrawn in September 1964. Another engine, No. 752 (Beyer Peacock No. 1989 of May 1881), is preserved and ran at the 1980 'Rainhill Cavalcade' when 99 years old. These facts are a tribute to Barton Wright's sound judgement and Aspinall's robust conversion.

J. B. Hodgson Collection

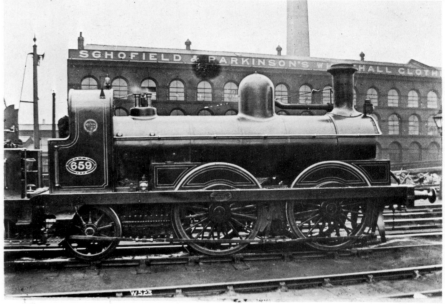

STATIONS

A series of contemporary photographs of Company stations taken at various times during their existence. The pictures are organized in counties and are in order of line opening.

LANCASHIRE STATIONS

Plate 88 The original, 1839, terminus of the Manchester & Leeds Railway at Oldham Road, photographed in the early 1900s. It became a goods yard after the line was extended to Hunts Bank in 1844 and was eventually demolished in 1968. In later years the roof was altered somewhat which spoilt the appearance of the building. The visible wagon is a Diagram 15 three plank dropside wagon with the Company 'Illiterate' symbol.

National Railway Museum

Plate 89 Holme Station, opened 1849, on the Todmorden to Burnley branch of the Manchester & Leeds Railway. This view is taken from the steps of the signal cabin around 1914, after the down platform had been rebuilt following an accident in 1907 when some runaway coke wagons from Copy Pit came crashing through the station, demolishing the buildings and taking the life of the relief station-master. The station closed in 1930 *(see also Plate 49)*.

F. W. Shuttleworth Collection

Plates 90 and 91 Two views of Helmshore Station on the East Lancashire Railway's alpine route from Stubbins to Accrington. *Plate 90* is the view towards Bury and Manchester with a train just disappearing. The idea of the canopy sheltering passengers, as part of the main building roof, was peculiar to the E L R. *Plate 91* shows the view in the Accrington direction. The goods facilities consisted of mill sidings to the left and a normal shed and yard complex to the right. There is also the opportunity to view the level crossing gates and the passenger footbridge with public access; an L & Y addition. The down platform canopy displays the L & Y quirk of painting the boarding alternate brown and lake. At least three styles of gas lamp are visible including some of an interesting squat design on the footbridge. The station staff are all lined up and the local Historical Society have discovered that the lady peering through the gate is Miss Lizzie Ingham. The station opened in 1849 and was closed, with the line, in 1966. At the time of writing, 1982, this was the last surviving East Lancashire Railway passenger building.

J. Peden Collection and Author's Collection

Plate 92 Accrington Station, the hub of the East Lancashire Railway's network, around 1912. The old stone-base signal box is just visible in this view taken from the Blackburn line platform looking towards Burnley. Standard signal brackets support the platform canopy as this part of the station was erected by the L & Y. Strangely, the room signs are enamelled and not the usual raised wood letters. Also of interest is the heavy six-legged station seat which seemed to abound on ex-E L R stations.

Author's Collection

Plate 93 This station has been included as it is the first station which I got to know, and travel from, and apart from the signals and adverts, the station had not changed very much by the late 1950s. The 'Barracks' part of the name referred to a nearby cavalry establishment and the station was the terminus of the first railway into Burnley in September 1848, before extending across the viaduct to Bank Top. The photograph dates from the early 1900s when the L&Y still used vertical bars on its distant signals instead of the later chevrons. The building behind and above, with paired windows, was a public house called 'The Lancashire and Yorkshire Railway Hotel' but it had no connection with the Railway Company. Hemmed in by bridges and buildings, I always felt it to be a typical urban station.

Author's Collection

Plate 94 Ormskirk Station, half-way house on the East Lancashire Railway's Liverpool, Ormskirk and Preston Railway section. Everyone, including another photographer, has turned out for this pre-Great War picture to view the arrival of the railmotor. The station was the junction for the line to Skelmersdale and on to Rainford and, in 1913, became the final terminus of the electric line from Liverpool.

P. Gibb Collection

Plate 95 Skelmersdale, with a coal train shunting into the goods yard which lies behind the camera. The East Lancashire pattern of ornate chimneys on station buildings has been perpetuated on to the brickwork. Closure of this station was in 1956.

P. Gibb Collection

Plate 96 Preston Road, the first separate station out of Exchange on the Liverpool to Bury Railway, opened in November 1848 and became part of the direct Manchester to Liverpool line. It was a small suburban station with numerous L&Y standard additions, including footbridge and bracket globular gas lamps which, like all L&Y station lamps on or near the platforms, carried the station name painted on the glass.

Author's Collection

Plate 97 Wigan in the rain, on 17th November 1913. Symptomatic of all that is Lancashire and its railway stations. The line of goods wagons comprises 'Lanky' standard type and private owner vehicles. The bay platform was known as a 'lighting up' bay from the days when a rake of oil-lit carriages would receive their pot lamps for the evening duties. The station seats are typical L&Y ornate traceries whilst also on the platform are two types of barrow peculiar to the L&Y. On the right, is a large wheeled platform barrow and to the left is a high trolley.

National Railway Museum

Plate 98 The 'Wigan' Orrell Station which was situated close to the summit of the four mile climb out of Wigan. The station featured a substantial covered footbridge and some new buildings at road level in the L&Y's yellow and purple-grey brick. The standard station nameboard, with its raised wooden letters, is seen to good effect against the cutting. It has a black background with letters and surround in white. The wooden supports are in the carriage tan colour and are the result of the station-master's personal whim.

P. Gibb Collection

Plates 99 and 100 Two views of Ainsdale on the Liverpool, Crosby & Southport Railway, showing both the rail and road views. Electrified in 1904, this station is largely without the quantity of specialist boards applicable to this electric line. *Plate 99* also shows a standard large wheel platform barrow, and a delightful perambulator, whilst *Plate 100* shows the footbridge and piecemeal additions of buildings. It also shows that not all roads were, by any means, 'made up'. The position of the signal ladder, sideways, was peculiar to, and a result of, the location.

P. Gibb Collection

Plate 101 Great Harwood Station, on the North Lancashire loop from Rose Grove to Blackburn, opened on 15th October 1877. One feature of this station was the ornate platform canopy boarding, and the external barge boarding on the road side of the station building. Standard signal brackets again support the canopy and amongst the general railway paraphernalia is an advert for the Midland Railway, which used nearby Blackburn. Opposite this station building stood a large wooden carriage shed housing several sidings which served the Blackburn area. The loop line remained open for many years after the withdrawal of passenger services in 1957.

A. Wilkinson Collection

Plate 102 Crossens was on the West Lancashire Railway, (Southport to Preston), and opened in 1878, but the arrival of the electrics in 1904 caused minor rebuilding to take place. Some new buildings and installations were added and the platform was surfaced with cross-hatched purple grey bricks. The gas light and notices are standard L & Y items. This was the terminus of the seventeen electric trains which ran express from Liverpool to Southport Chapel Street and then on to Crossens. Trains to Preston were steam-hauled. This view of the station was taken on 12th March 1912.

National Railway Museum

Plate 103 Halsall Station on the line from Southport to Altcar and Hillhouse opened in September 1887, a line which became a home for the railmotors, the service starting in December 1909 becoming known locally as the 'Altcar Bob'. The line ran through agricultural land and never generated much traffic, other than seasonable vegetable, and the building of the line virtually bankrupted the West Lancashire Railway. Passenger facilities ceased in September 1938 but goods traffic lasted until January 1952. The platforms are stone faced and edged, but with an ash infill. The house still survives but all else, save the road bridge, has disappeared. The station sat on one of the shallowest gradients on the L&Y (1 in 2,838). The locality abounded in pheasants and railmotor drivers and firemen often came home with 'a little extra' to supplement the family menu.

Author's Collection

Plate 104 Moorside & Wardley, a new island platform station built within the slow lines of the Hindley to Pemberton loop, south of Wigan, opened on 1st June 1889. The fast lines never served the station and they curve through the foreground. The station is typical of L&Y island platforms of the period. The nameboard deserves comment as its construction is different from the standard style, (e.g. Crossens, *Plate 102*), using tenon joints.

Author's Collection

YORKSHIRE STATIONS

Plate 105 Hebden Bridge Station of Manchester & Leeds Railway origin, 1841, with the original station building still rising over the later canopy. At first, goods were catered for in the open-sided tranship shed, set at 45 degrees to the running lines and reached by a wagon turntable. The huge goods shed and warehouse came later, although even this was built in two stages. This photograph was taken at the heyday of the railway around 1910.

J. B. Hodgson Collection

Plate 106 Horbury Junction Station, an all wood structure, put in on the old Manchester & Leeds line, pictured at the turn of the century when the lines around the area, bounded by Wakefield, Woolley Tunnel and Thornhill were receiving considerable alteration and widening.

Author's Collection

Plate 107 Cleckheaton Station, on the former West Riding Union Railway, opened in May 1850. This picture shows the Midland Royal Train working towards Bradford. As this is not the Midland's Royal Train engine, and the locomotive, a 4-4-0, No. 495, only has three lamps instead of the four carried on Royal journeys, she must be hauling empty stock. A small boiler 0-8-0, with an interested crew, sit amidst various bits of 'Lanky' station furniture of which the loading gauge and telegraph pole are of the greatest interest.

J. B. Hodgson Collection

Plate 108 A view of Bradford Exchange Station, now, alas, no more. This station was jointly held with the Great Northern Railway. It was a terminal station which lay at the foot of a mile long 1 in 50 gradient with a four road bottleneck at its throat. E. L. Ahrons. who knew the station very well, wrote about the misfortunes which befell the earlier building almost lovingly but, like the L&Y itself, Bradford Exchange was altered out of all recognition. Completed in 1888, there were ten platforms instead of three, the longest taking twelve carriages, two 50 ft. turntables, a dining room and two beautiful arched canopies. A second series Atlantic, No. 1407 at platform 5, in May 1905, is about to depart for Manchester. Great Northern carriages are in platform 6.

B. C. Lane Collection

Plate 109 This view of Bradford Exchange Station has much to delight the eye. It was really taken for the sighting of signals, *(see also Plate 253)*, but one's attention is drawn to the construction of the overall roof, the platform water column, the gas lamps and, finally, the track with its check rails and experimental retarder. A 2-4-2T is about to depart with a local train, and the covered walkway to the Great Northern's Victoria Hotel is behind the railings. You can view this picture for a long time and still find new points of interest.

National Railway Museum

Plate 110 Brockholes Station on the Huddersfield & Sheffield Junction Railway opened on 1st July 1850. In this Edwardian view both enamel and wood letter signboards are visible. A set of platform steps is ready for Huddersfield-bound passengers and a platform trolley, with unusual disc wheels, is clearly visible.

P. Gibb Collection

When Aspinall transferred to the position of General Manager, his position as Chief Mechanical Engineer was filled by Harry Hoy. Aspinall's policies were continued by Hoy for a while, after which he began his own innovations which were, to say the least, a little strange at times. Some of his engines and experiments are shown in the following photographs but his major lasting contributions were the full lettering on locomotives and the fitting of eight wheel tenders to the 0-8-0s. Hoy resigned in 1904 to become General Manager at Beyer Peacock and his passing brought a few quiet sighs of relief. He was succeeded by George Hughes who was a sound designer and locomotive engineer whose ambition was to provide greater power and efficiency for locomotives. Although his genius did falter at times, it was his later locomotives which were better and ensured his reputation. He remained at the top of his profession for over twenty years, leaving behind him locomotives capable of tackling any job which the traffic department could give them. His final design, for the LMS Railway, not illustrated in this volume, was an adaptable mixed traffic 2-6-0 which gave forty years of excellent service. One wonders if the 'Crabs' might ever have appeared as L&Y engines. However, Hughes' locomotives were not just enlargements of Aspinall types, although he did extend these to the limits of their design. They were, as L&Y locomotives had been since the days of Barton Wright, rugged and well to the fore in standardization and innovation.

Plate 111 Hoy had only one original engine design constructed during his term of office. Twenty 2-6-2Ts were built in 1903/4 for the steeply graded, heavily loaded, Manchester to Oldham line and the branches to Bacup. They looked ungainly but they did fulfil their tasks. By the time the Hughes superheated 2-4-2Ts superseded them in 1913, they had gained a reputation for eating coal and leaking tanks, and they were relegated to shunting and banking jobs. For these, several alterations were made including the removal of the flanges from the centre drivers, and there were many instances of these coming 'off the road' to further malign their reputation. No. 387, shown here, was built in November 1903 (Works No. 862) and the photograph shows the additional smokebox door for ash and the thin taper chimney. The engine was withdrawn in 1925, as were most of the class, having ended its days at Rose Grove banking trains to Copy Pit.

J. B. Hodgson Collection

Plates 112 (right) and 113 (below) Hoy seemed to prefer experimenting or trying to improve already tried and trusted designs. One of his first efforts was on an Aspinall 4-4-0, No. 1112. *Plate 113* shows the engine in works grey livery whilst *Plate 112* is a front three-quarter view, displaying how the engine was made to resemble a LNWR 'Alfred the Great' class locomotive. Only the chimney and tender gave away its identity. The engine became a four cylinder Compound with a 200 p.s.i. boiler and it worked for some seven years in this condition before disappearing into Horwich Works to be rebuilt again as in *Plate 128*.

R. J. Hunter Collection and
J. B. Hodgson Collection

Plate 114 (top)   Following the accident to 0-8-0, No. 676, at Knottingley *(Plate 84)*, Hoy designed a stay-less circular firebox for the 0-8-0s. Twenty one engines were built with these fireboxes, in 1903, and they ran for about ten years with them before being converted to large boiler engines. They were difficult to get into steam as the boilers scaled badly and they eventually worked out of true, needing jacking back into place at Horwich. Again, no real measure of success was achieved and the class gained the appalling nickname 'Sea Pigs'. No. 408 is pictured at Low Moor on 15th July 1905.

J. B. Hodgson Collection

Plates 115 (middle) and 116 (bottom)   Another peculiar Hoy adaptation was the Druitt-Halpin thermal storage tank, which must be high on the list as the most ungainly locomotive adornment of all time. It was an attempt to supply warm, or already hot, water directly into the boiler at times of excessive effort, thus saving fuel in heating and preventing excessive expansion and contraction of pipework. The first engine was converted in 1902 but No. 1375, pictured here, did not receive hers until 1905, in Hughes' days. The apparatus was not a great success as on level ground it showed hardly any saving. The internal pipes scaled up badly and around 1911 it was removed. No. 1375 was an Accrington engine for much of the period, but is pictured here, at Low Moor, on 15th July 1905. Of amusing interest is the handlamp on the cab roof, situated there for illuminating a gauge glass on the tank.

J. B. Hodgson Collection

Plate 117 One of Hughes' first changes, when he became Chief Mechanical Engineer, was to further improve the 2-4-2Ts. In this case, a saturated Belpaire boiler, with 40 per cent more steam space and 20 per cent more water space, was fitted along with a separate extended smokebox on a cast saddle. No. 1461 was the eleventh locomotive completed, and on 27th July 1905 she was turned out still with the Hoy lettering style on the curve. In later years many round top engines received Belpaire boilers and looked very much like this. This photograph of No. 1461 was taken at Poulton.

The late J. M. Tomlinson

Plate 118 In order to combat the encroaching electric tramways which were already affecting revenue on local services, Hughes designed a cheap, light, easily worked modern unit whose speed might win back the customers. This was a combination of a diminutive engine and a single coach and was termed 'rail motor'. Two units bought from Kerr Stuart inaugurated the service and the Hughes design soon appeared in May 1906. The units were, actually, separate entities which could be broken up and different pairs assembled whenever repairs were necessary. The photograph deals largely with engine No. 16, (both units had their own number series), one of three built in 1909 and it features the wide chimney and dogged smokebox door which these locomotives latterly received. The location is Southport Chapel Street with a proud crew of driver, fireman and guard who was also a ticket inspector and general jack of all trades where these services were concerned. The driver drove from the footplate and an end driving compartment, *(see Plate 159)*, connected to the engine by a system of wires and levers.

Author's Collection

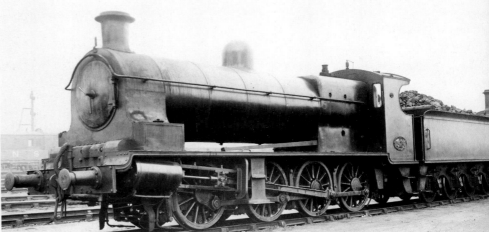

Plates 120 and 121   The results of compounding on a passenger locomotive *(Plates 112/3)*, were not at all successful, but Hughes decided the system might be advantageous for goods work. He selected 0-8-0, No. 1452, and arranged the 15½in. high pressure cylinders outside and the 22in. low pressure cylinders inside, each to drive the second axle. *Plate 120* shows a front view of No. 1452 in Horwich Works yard in February 1906. Up to July 1906, a 25 per cent saving on coal was effected and instructions were given to build twenty new Compounds. In the end only ten were completed (Nos. 1471-1480), the others being Simples. One or two detail differences were made which are shown in *Plate 121*. Firstly, there was divided drive where the high pressure cylinders drove the third axle and the low pressure ones, inside, drove the second axle. The footplate was upswept to clear all wheels and motion. Finally a new wide chimney was introduced on these locomotives. The engines were quite successful but, if anything, short of boiler power. No. 1474, shown here, was turned out on 4th May 1907 and worked from Agecroft. It was eventually discovered that the coal saving was not sufficient to cover the extra initial cost of manufacture, nor the extra maintenance necessary and no more were built. All were withdrawn in 1926/7.   *National Railway Museum and Real Photographs*

◁ *Plate 119*   Hughes' answer to the traffic department's request for a heavy shunting and banking locomotive which could shift virtually anything were the massive 0-8-2Ts completed in March/April 1908. The 'Little Egberts', as they were nicknamed after a local troupe of performing circus elephants, were the first application of a large boiler to an eight-coupled engine. They were not standard, having a different wheelbase, some flangeless driving wheels, oval buffers and wheel lock smokebox door mechanism amongst their peculiarities, but they were successful in their work. This photograph shows No. 1504 at Aintree hauling a coal train in the yards on 26th April 1911.

National Railway Museum

Plate 122   This shows a rear three-quarter view of No. 1502 at Accrington, waiting near the Blackburn to Manchester lines to bank a southbound train to Baxenden. The layout of coal rails, rear step, handrail and bunker lining can all be seen. No. 1504 was the last of these locomotives to be withdrawn in October 1929.

B. C. Lane Collection

Plate 123 The Hughes 4-6-0s, as first conceived, were meant to be the flagships of the fleet but, in spite of the careful thinking that went into them, they were sluggish runners and poor steamers, or otherwise, heavy on coal. Twenty were turned out between June 1908 and March 1909 to handle the increased weight of trains such as the Liverpool to Hull expresses and the Leeds-Bradford-Fleetwood boat trains. The traffic department, however, had wanted the engines too soon as a couple of years later, with additional experience in superheating, a different engine would have emerged to enhance, not malign, Hughes' reputation. No. 1511 (Works No. 1014) is seen at York. The bogie brakes were removed around 1914.

J. B. Hodgson Collection

Plate 124 Hughes also tried his hand at improving earlier designs. His attempt at the 0-6-0 goods engines culminated in twenty being built with Belpaire boilers, various types of superheater and 20½in. cylinders. Other outward differences included larger cabs and bigger sandboxes beside the smokebox. These engines were coupled to heavier tenders which acquired double springs. No. 657 was the first of these engines built, (Works No. 1152 of 5th March 1912), and was fitted with the Schmidt superheater.

Author's Collection

Plate 125   In improving the 0-8-0s, Hughes first tried the larger boiler used on the 4-6-0s and then introduced superheating using several different types. Eventually one hundred and five superheated and forty saturated engines were built. No. 1569, pictured here, was part of Lot 71, turned out on 16th August 1913, and was fitted with the Horwich Twin Plug superheater. The engines ran with eight wheel tenders but the photograph shows a ROD tender (GC type) coupled for comparative purposes to No. 1569 as it passed through the shops early in 1920. The idea was to assess their suitability for use on the L & Y and some were eventually used, with new 4-6-0s, in modified form.

National Railway Museum

Plate 126 (right)   No. 2, photographed here at Sandhills, was one of the three Simplex petrol tractors purchased in 1920 for work in Great Howard Street goods yard, Liverpool. Fitted with 30 h.p. 4 cylinder engines, the gearboxes gave three speeds in both directions. Like the railmotors and electric locomotives, these engines were numbered in their own series and, with their split spoke wheels and steeple cabs, appeared very quaint.

Real Photographs

Plate 127   Hughes knew his 4-6-0 required some alteration and there is some evidence that, but for the Great War, this would have taken place sooner. However, it was 1920 before these locomotives could be revamped resulting in a major transformation. With superheaters, redesigned steam passages, Walschaert's valve gear and long lap piston valves these engines became masters of their work. Because of the new cylinders and outside steam pipes the opportunity was taken to clean up the design and a much more balanced looking engine resulted. No. 1509 is pictured at Agecroft.

A. G. Ellis Collection

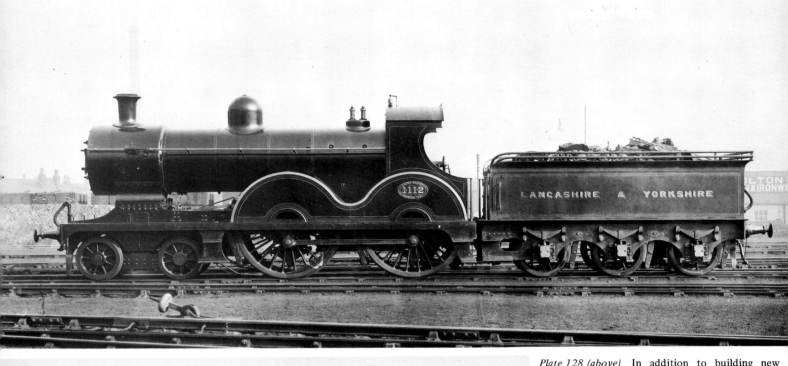

Plate 128 (above) In addition to building new types and improving former designs Hughes, like his predecessors, also tried his hand at rebuilding engines and one of the first was No. 1112 (see Plate 113). She reappeared in December 1908 in the form illustrated here. A 2 cylinder Simple, round top boiler with Ross 'pop' safety-valves and Schmidt superheater, extended smokebox on a cast steel saddle, taper chimney and Joy valve gear. In this form she resembled No. 1110 (Plate 7). The engine steamed well and gave a reasonable coal economy. No. 1112 was also given an experimental lining of one thin red and one thin white line, whilst the tender, with normal lining, had rounded corners not inset ones, and this is the livery shown photographed, on 9th February 1909. She was to be rebuilt again, in 1918, with a Belpaire boiler, appearing similar to No. 1221 which is seen in Plate 29.

National Railway Museum

Plates 129 (left) and 130 (below) Hughes rebuilt many Aspinall engines with Belpaire boilers and, in some cases, superheaters. *Plate 129* shows 2-4-2T, No. 76 (built 21st March 1896), and which was reboilered in August 1915, at Salford with the 1922 style livery. The class plate '5' is on the cabside and the shed plate '21' (Bacup) at the rear of the cab. *Plate 130* shows 0-6-0 No. 453 (built 15th October 1900) also fitted with a Belpaire boiler, on this occasion in May 1920 when a superheater was also fitted. A comparison with *Plate 124* will show the external detail differences. Both engines survived into BR days.

A. G. Ellis Collection and
B. C. Lane Collection

Plate 131 This photograph shows the final alterations made by Hughes to the Atlantics with extended smokebox and new dogged door resting on a cast steel saddle. Here, No. 1406 leaves York with a Manchester bound express.

J. B. Hodgson Collection

Plate 132 No. 731 was Hughes' 'pet' engine and was the last survivor of the Ramsbottom Newtons purchased from the LNWR in 1873. This engine was drafted on to hauling the CME's saloon in 1886, which was the combined bogie tender and saloon device shown in this picture. The latter had a vibration of its own. Apparently, the only truly comfortable seat, which Hughes took, was in one of the corners where his back was to the engine. By the time this photograph was taken, around 1921, the engine was on her third boiler. A parallel chimney and closed splashers had also radically altered her appearance from the early days. This unique combination, with George Hughes chatting to the footplate crew, is pictured at Manchester Victoria.

The late G. W. Smith

ENGINEERING FEATURES

Like all railways, and more than most, the L&Y had a vast quantity and variety of bridges, tunnels, viaducts and retaining walls of many differing types and styles, often the legacy of the original local company. There were 91 tunnels and 2,478 under and over bridges over the 585 route miles of line.

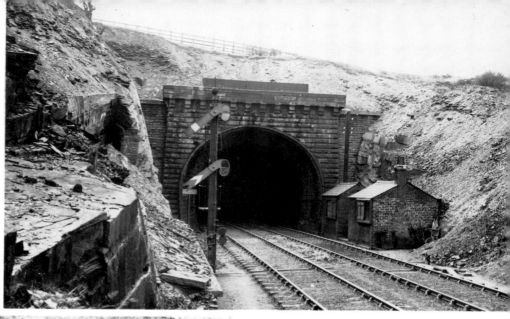

TUNNELS

Plates 133 to 136 Four double track tunnels of varying profiles are shown in the following photographs. In *Plate 133*, Up Holland Tunnel (959 yards) is typical of the L&Y layout of tunnel gang's hut and paraphernalia, signals and name board. This view shows the east portal. *Plate 134* is the magnificently designed and dressed west portal of Summit Tunnel, the longest 'Lanky' tunnel at 2,885 yards, and this also shows the fog signalman's hut. *Plate 135* is Kirkdale No. 2 Tunnel, a pair of double track bores. One new bore was driven in the 1890s as part of a widening scheme in that area. This is the Liverpool end of the 210 yard tunnel and is an LMS picture as the distants are now painted yellow and sighting boards have been provided. *Plate 136* is Holme Tunnel (265 yards) on the Todmorden to Burnley line looking up to Copy Pit from the station.

P. Gibb Collection and the late J. M. Tomlinson

BRIDGES

Plate 137 Chatham Bridge, between Portsmouth and Copy Pit, on the Todmorden to Burnley line, seen at the time when the up loop was being constructed in 1906. The architects have taken care to blend the new bridge in with its neighbour. The contractor's wagons, (Thomas Wrigley), are very interesting and the L&Y permanent way and ballast are well shown.

J. B. Hodgson Collection

VIADUCTS

Plates 138 and 139 The Aspen Viaduct lies between Rishton and Church & Oswaldtwistle stations on the former East Lancashire line. This single track structure crosses some very unstable ground and, as built, was probably the only means of surmounting the obstacle. It survived an attempt, in 1847, by a clumsy carpenter, to burn it down with a shovelful of lighted shavings. He was more interested in his own warmth and he lost his bothy but the viaduct was saved. With the increases in traffic it became a bottleneck and several schemes were devised to turn it into a plain double track viaduct. However, being wooden, and 70 ft. high, it shook a little as trains passed over causing passengers some apprehension. Eventually, it was decided to bury the viaduct, many thinking it a plain embankment, not realizing what is beneath the trestle, in all its glory, before tipping commenced. The ash from locomotive fires and smokeboxes was used to create the embankment and this arrived from all over the L&Y system for the Sunday ritual of shovelling it over the edge. This continued until 1927 when they finally reached rail level and created a top wide enough to take the double track. *Plate 139* shows the state of affairs early in LMS days. Rail travellers between the two stations still travel over the viaduct, many thinking it a plain embankment, not realizing what is beneath the wheels of their train.

J. B. Hodgson Collection and
P. Gibb Collection

Plates 140 to 142   Many early railways received timber trestle viaducts and *Plate 140* shows Hawkshaw's timber viaduct at Denby Dale being replaced by a new stone structure in 1884. It was Company policy to eliminate all such timber structures by one means or another as soon as practicable. *Plate 141* shows Swanside Viaduct at Rimington on the Blackburn to Hellifield line, and being in limestone country, the twelve arch viaduct was constructed in the local stone. In the photograph, a 2-4-2T, with a local train, heads for Hellifield. *Plate 142* shows the north end of the Whalley Viaduct of 48 brick spans and always known locally as Whalley Arches. Two of the centre spans have a gothic church window style of infill built to suit the nearby grounds of the local abbey, an old religious centre close to the River Calder over which the railway passes. This old postcard also shows the L&Y style of telegraph pole with alternate short and long arms, and the method of fixing to the viaduct side.

T. Wray Collection, V. R. Anderson Collection and Author's Collection

Plate 141

Plate 142

RIVER AND ROAD BRIDGES

Plates 143 and 144 The bridge over the River Douglas on the West Lancashire Railway's Southport to Preston line. The Act of Parliament declared that it had to be a swing bridge to allow the river to remain navigable to shipping. *Plate 143* shows the bridge on test whilst *Plate 144* shows flooding of the surrounding fields following storms in March 1908. Of great interest is the telegraph pole next to the bridge with its tremendous height giving clearance to ships. The excessive timbering was to prevent damage to the bridge piers.

P. Gibb Collection

Plate 144

Plate 145 Bridges over roads were commonplace and here is an ornate example in the park at Preston, where the Blackburn line out of the station crossed over the public amenity. The East Lancashire Railway built this skew arch with balustrade, thus producing the ultimate promenade diversion. The bridge was also used as the headshunt for the goods yard and often carried a locomotive. Here, the locomotive, No. 602 *Roach*, a Yates 4 ft. 0 in. saddle tank of March 1875 and a replacement for an ex-EL engine, *(see also Plate 45)*, but with the plain sheet cab, is seen on the bridge. The locomotive was withdrawn in January 1898.

A. G. Ellis Collection

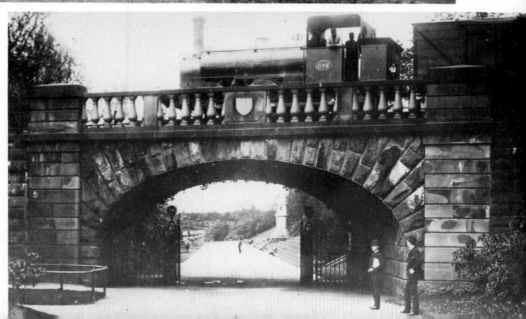

CARRIAGES AND NON-PASSENGER COACHING STOCK

L&Y carriage design followed that of many other companies, commencing with four wheel and then six wheel rigid vehicles before progressing to bogie vehicles of many different types. However, L&Y policy was to convert the old four and six wheelers to non-passenger coaching stock to obtain extra use from them. Thus almost the whole carriage building history of the L&Y was on view to the end of the Company's life. The ensuing story has been taken out of sequence so that the use of the older rigid stock as non-passenger coaching stock vehicles can be portrayed at the end of the section.

Carriages and wagons were built and rebuilt at the works at Newton Heath which had been opened in 1877. Around that time the Carriage & Wagon Superintendent, Charles Fay, who had joined the M&L in that capacity in 1846, retired through ill health and Mr F. Attock succeeded to the post and began designing the arc roof style of carriage which was to epitomise the L&Y for many years. *Plate 47* has already described the earlier Fay style and design.

Attock resigned for health reasons in 1895, and in 1899 the overall responsibility passed to the CME, although the title 'Carriage & Wagon Superintendent' was retained, first by G. Banks to 1909 and then by F. E. Gobey. Banks began the move to elliptical roofs but it was Gobey who really spread their use.

L&Y carriage stock, in 1921, totalled 4,360, which comprised 2,983 single class vehicles, 789 composites, 4 restaurant cars and 584 others, (non-passenger coaching stock).

Plate 146   This shows carriage No. 846, an eight compartment 1st/2nd, one of seventy five carriages built in several lots to Diagram 45. It is very typical of the Attock style of carriage and became known as the '1900 Standard'. It has the standard doors and windows fitted to four, six and eight wheel carriages, from 1877 to the Great War period. There are torpedo vents on every compartment, although there are only two 'smoking' compartments. This vehicle shows the Coligny gas lights used in 1st Class compartments. The carriage, 54 ft. 0 in. long and 8 ft. 6 in. wide, seated sixty four passengers and rode on the transverse and lateral-spring 8 ft. 0 in. wheelbase standard bogie. As 2nd Class was abolished in 1912, the compartments would then be designated 3rd Class.   *National Railway Museum*

Plate 147 (middle)   Carriage No. 3290 was ordered (M28) in 1912 as an experimental ten compartment all 3rd vehicle meant for one hundred and twenty passengers. It cost £898 7s 8d and was ascribed to Diagram 142. At 60 ft. 0 in. long, it became part of the only batch of L&Y eight wheel carriages longer than 56 ft. 0 in. The width was 9 ft. 0 in. and the 10 ft. 0 in. wheelbase wide bearing bogie was fitted. The smaller gas lamps of the later elliptical roofed stock were the means of lighting. Evidently, the carriage was a success, as a further twenty were ordered on 29th January 1913 but, owing to the Great War conditions, these were not built until 1920/21 when raging inflation pushed the cost up to exactly £2,000 per vehicle. Thus, the type became the ultimate compartment carriage design. As a reflection on social change since 1900, half the compartments are now designated 'smoking'.   *National Railway Museum*

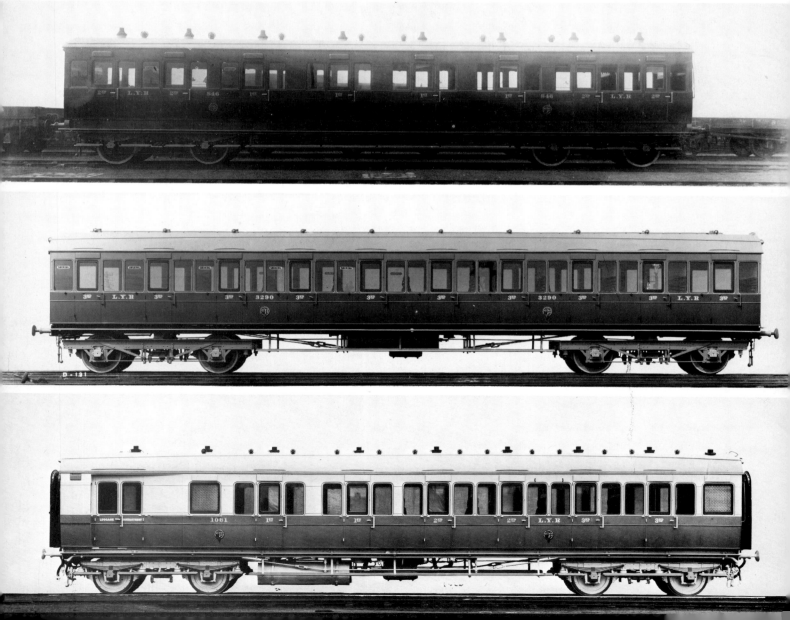

Plates 148 (lower left) and 149 (above) Booking from the L&Y, it was possible to reach any one of four London termini; King's Cross (via Wakefield), St. Pancras (from Blackburn via Manchester Victoria), Marylebone (from Bradford and Halifax via Sheffield) and Euston (from Colne via Manchester Victoria and Stockport, and from Southport). There were also through carriages to Glasgow, Harrogate and other cities. In all, twenty three elliptical roof brake composites were built for such services. *Plate 148* shows No. 1061, a dual fitted corridor tri-composite of 1907 (Lot K23 and Diagram 84). There were ten built in this first batch, the only tri-style. Subsequent batches, built up to 1914, were 1st/3rd only. No. 1061 was 56ft. 0in. long, 9ft. 0in. wide and fitted with the standard 8ft. 0in. wheelbase bogie. This 'Lot' had the high Pope gas lights which prevented their use on the Midland Railway and on all Scottish railways. The photograph shows the vehicle in works grey. In reality the two colours of the livery at this time, purple brown lower panels and buff above, were hardly distinguishable in photographs because of the orthochromatic emulsions used. This style of carriage also introduced the inset end, an arrangement to allow the guard to look out down the length of the train without using extra width, which resulted in passengers obtaining the full benefit of the width allowed by loading gauge. It was later applied to all brake carriages and became a distinctive L&Y feature. *Plate 149* shows a well known Midland Railway picture with the leading vehicle being one of the later through composites. This 1st/3rd has altered lavatory windows, lower gas lights and 10ft. 0in. wheelbase wide bearing bogies.

National Railway Museum and B. C. Lane Collection

DINING SERVICES

Plates 150 (above), 151 (top overleaf) and 152 (bottom overleaf) With few long runs of any note, especially those allowing time to serve a meal, L&Y dining services were rather infrequent. It was not until 1901 that a kitchen was actually fitted into a L&Y carriage, initial use being on the Leeds to Fleetwood boat train. *Plate 150* shows carriage No. 200, one of two 1st Class saloons ordered in 1900 to Diagram 46. Each was 52ft. 0in. long, 9ft. 0in. wide and ran on 8ft. 0in. wheelbase transverse bogies. It was typical of the short lived intermediate period when panelled carriages became the vogue and the carriage was fitted with recessed doors at the ends. There were droplights at each table, Coligny gas lamps were fitted and there were thirteen body brackets per solebar. No. 200 was the dining saloon used in conjunction with the famous ten wheel kitchen 2nd brake No. 3, at the right of the picture, and these worked the boat train until 1907. *Plate 151* shows the interior of No. 200 a little later when the 'smoking' section had been extended. The lavishness of the interior can be seen along with 'LYR' in the antimacassars, and timetables are provided for the CR, NER, H&BR and G&SWR. *Plate 152* is a magnesium flash picture of the chef at work in the kitchen of dining car No. 215 (Order No. M26 of 5th November 1909 and given Diagram 120). Interior provisions were similar in all twelve wheel 1st Class dining cars. Cooking was by gaslights on a gas range supplied by Fletcher Russell of Warrington. They were lined with sheet aluminium and there was a crude sink, wooden drainer and slate chopping board along with various cupboards. The kitchen served not only the 1st Class diners in Car No. 215, but also an adjoining 3rd Class vehicle. No. 215 generally worked the Hull to Liverpool service.

J. B. Hodgson Collection and National Railway Museum

Plate 151

THE CLUB CARRIAGE

Plates 153 (top right) and 154 (bottom right
Carriage No. 47 was a bogie vestibule 1st Clas
(of course), carriage for the Blackpool t
Manchester service and which replaced tw
earlier arc roofed vehicles. Built in 1912 to Orde
E28 and given Diagram 126, it was 58 ft. 0 in. long
9 ft. 0 in. wide and was fitted with the 10 ft. 0 in
wheelbase wide bearing bogies. Wide pictur
windows were installed, developed from the dinin
cars and railmotors, and only one central door pe
side. However, it seated only forty passengers, th
forty members of the 'Club', an organization o
Manchester businessmen who lived in Blackpoo
and travelled to work on the same train each day
the 8.10 a.m. from Blackpool, returning home o
the 5.10 p.m. from Manchester. Here was tota
exclusivity as the carriage was built just for th
'Club' members. There were armchairs through
out, thirty were for smokers. It had occasiona
tables, an attendant to serve tea and the 'Club' had
its own rules of membership, which was by
election only. *Plate 154* shows the original interio
layout. The carriage was always marshalled as the
second carriage in, at the Manchester end of the
train, at the request of the members. Around 191
the vehicle received some minor alterations a
Newton Heath Works, including the fitting o
electric lighting and a slightly rearranged interio
layout, possibly to provide better conditions fo
card playing. *Plate 153* shows the external view
of No. 47 in its converted form when it was given
a new Diagram No. 143.

National Railway Museur

Plate 152

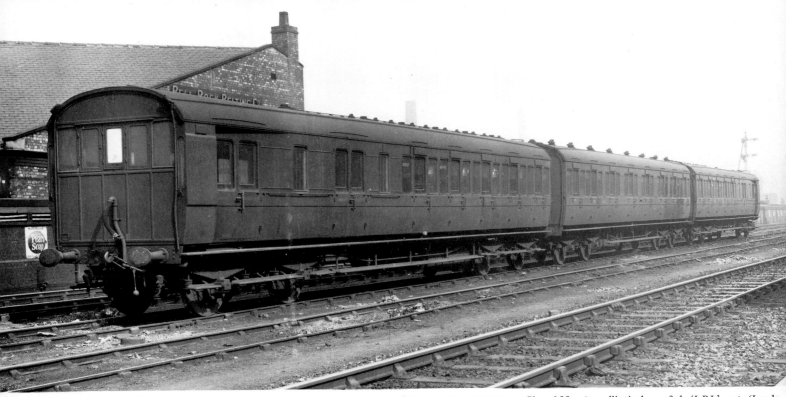

Plate 155 An elliptical roofed 'LBL' set (Leeds-Bradford-Liverpool). This comprised three carriages, always fixed as two brake (or van) 3rds with a 1st/2nd composite between. In a set like this, (two 54 ft. 0 in. 3rds and a 56 ft. 0 in. composite), there were seats for 198 passengers (30 x 1st Class, 48 x 2nd Class and 120 x 3rd Class). The inset ends are to the fore as is the white central end window, a L&Y practice described in *Plate 23*. Although known as 'LBL' sets, they were never confined exclusively to such services and were used all over the system. Trains could be made up from one, two or even three such sets with strengthening vehicles added as traffic demanded. This particular set was photographed in the carriage sidings on the approach to Manchester on 15th September 1915.

National Railway Museum

Plate 156 The interior of a 1st Class compartment of carriage No. 1085 which was one of a series of twelve 1st/3rd, 56 ft. 0 in. composites ordered in March 1912, to Lot F28, and which became part of Diagram 130. The interior is typical of the time. All woodwork was polished mahogany with polished brass metal fittings. The heavily buttoned floral pattern upholstery was introduced during the Edwardian era and such marks of luxury such as the leather trim, linen antimacassars and carpet, incorporating the weaving in of the Company crest, were at their peak at this time. Most 1st Class passengers had access to a toilet which, on these vehicles, was shared with the next door compartment. The door to the toilet can be seen at the left rear of the picture which was taken on 19th November 1912.

National Railway Museum

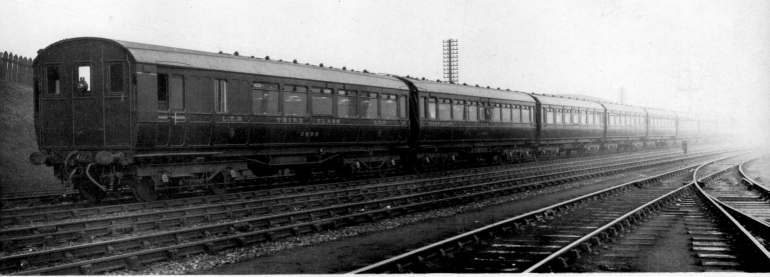

Plate 157 The disastrous fires at Aisgill and Mallerstang, on the Midland Railway, caused by gas escaping after accidents, raised such an outcry that George Hughes, still intent on using gas, designed the 'fireproof' trains for the L&Y. Three types of carriage were built; brake 3rd, full 3rd and full 1st and all were to the (now usual) open centre gangway pattern. The bodies were of steel with wooden mouldings, whilst the floors were faced on both sides with asbestos. The gas cylinders were jacketed with steel and provided with automatic cut-out valves to ensure no escape of gas in the event of a fracture. Two trains entered service on the Manchester to Southport line in 1913, and this photograph shows one of these with brake 3rd, No. 3288 (Diagram 131), full 3rd, No. 3300 and full 1st, No. 187. All had Hughes wide bearing 10 ft. 0 in. wheelbase bogies with inside springs. The brakes were the only ones ever fitted with three lights in the end instead of five. In 1917, further stock was built, including five 1st/3rd composites, but the brake 3rds were fitted with corridor gangways in the ends. All the stock lasted into BR days although it was converted to electric lighting by the LMS.

National Railway Museum

Plate 158 A L&Y toilet, of 1912, showing the fittings which were typical of corridor elliptical roofed carriages of the time. The enamelled wall covering was used extensively with walls, ceiling and cistern being covered and the water pipes are finished to match. On the left, and outside, can be seen a water filter to provide 'germproof' drinking water. This was a standard fixture in most L&Y corridor carriages of the time.

National Railway Museum

Plates 159 and 160 Railmotor carriage No. 13 which, at the time these photographs were taken, November 1920, could have been attached to any of the eighteen locomotive portions *(see Plate 118)*. When the carriages were built, the end was fully glazed but trailer cars were soon deemed necessary and all carriages eventually had the vestibule corridor connection fitted. The conversions were made at around the time that the last batch was built, in 1911, and those too may have been built new to that form. Folding steps were available for halts and low platformed stations, but were not required here, at Southport St. Luke's. Alas the photographs were taken to illustrate how one unfortunate passenger fell into the gap between the carriage and platform. The well weathered livery can be seen to advantage in *Plate 160*. The mouldings are edged in pale orange and the gold leaf numbers and lettering have a white outer line. However, the orthochromatic film cannot distinguish between the 'lake' lower panels and the tan upper ones. As with many such views, there is much to interest the reader in addition to the main subject of the picture.

National Railway Museum

Plates 161 and 162 On most pre-group railways, the practice of 'slipping' carriages from express trains was a short-lived phenomenon. This method of detachment of an additional portion from the train was particularly suited to the L&Y with its numerous junctions and connecting services, and allowed the train to continue unhindered. Drivers were instructed to maintain 30 m.p.h. whilst the 'slip' was taking place, and the separate guard had a lever to release the train coupling, a valve to apply the vacuum brakes and a handbrake wheel for general or emergency use. *Plate 162* shows the internal appointments and must be directly related to the features shown in *Plate 161*. Normal compartment stock was converted for 'slip' working of which carriage No. 1722, shown here, was one of 349 brake 3rds built, between 1899 and 1905, to Diagram 42. A composite carriage was usually paired with the 'slip' brake 3rd in order to provide all three classes within the 'slip' portion. Also visible is the fixed gas lamp in front of the white panel which was controlled from within the guard's compartment, the coloured glass on the ducket lit from an oil lamp within which would show red to the rear and green to the fore and, because this is a 'slip' carriage, a sand pipe to aid in braking the 'slip' portion. Adverse weather conditions would cause the 'slip' to be cancelled and the train would stop in the appropriate station for normal detachment of the 'slip' portion. These views were photographed in October 1913.

National Railway Museum

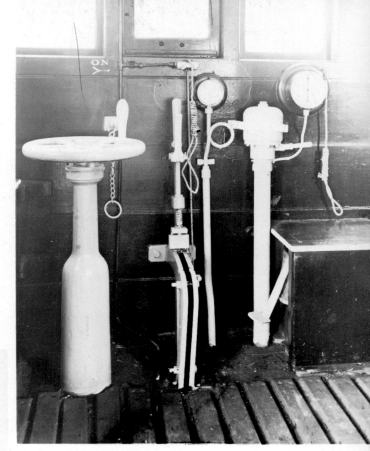

Plate 161

Plate 162

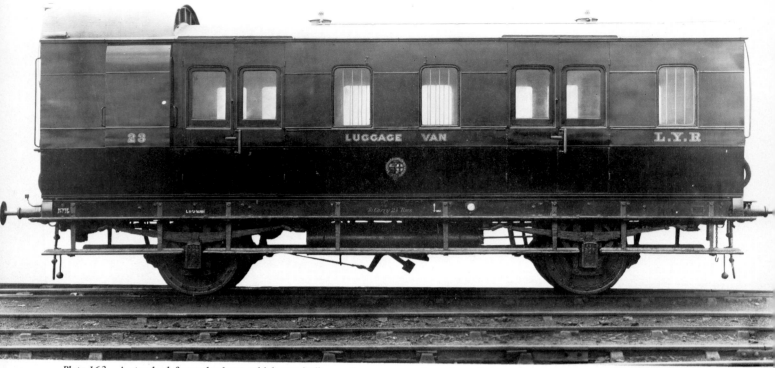

Plate 163 A standard four wheel van which was built as a luggage van and was later designated Diagram 1. Built early in Attock's career, it embodies some of the features which he introduced, such as the profiling, the smooth unpanelled sides and the inward step below waist level. With a length of 27 ft. 6 in, the type was multiplied up to about 80 units. In this 1917 picture, the van has been modified and yet has retained its full birdcage. Gas lighting has replaced the original oil lamps. The type was a natural successor to Fay's previous designs and a set of carriages usually had one of these vans at one end of the train. Some of the vans were still in use on breakdown trains at the end of the LMS period.

National Railway Museum

Plate 164 This was a standard Attock three compartment 3rd brake of the 1880s. It was built in large numbers and was the type most commonly altered or converted to the various different types of truck or van favoured by the L&Y. The conversion involved the fixing of the doors of the 1st and 3rd compartments and providing of double doors in the centre compartment. The interior was gutted and bars were fitted to the inside of all fixed windows and to the droplights of the old doors. Gas lamps were fitted in the standard van positions. The steps were altered and a handbrake lever was provided as these vans could also work in goods trains. They retained their 33 ft. 0 in. length and were in use well into the 1930s.

National Railway Museum

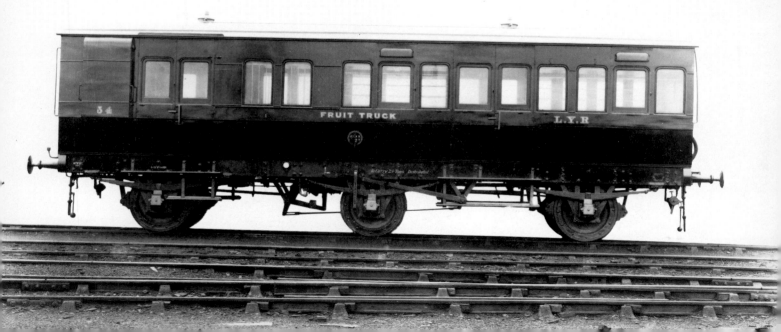

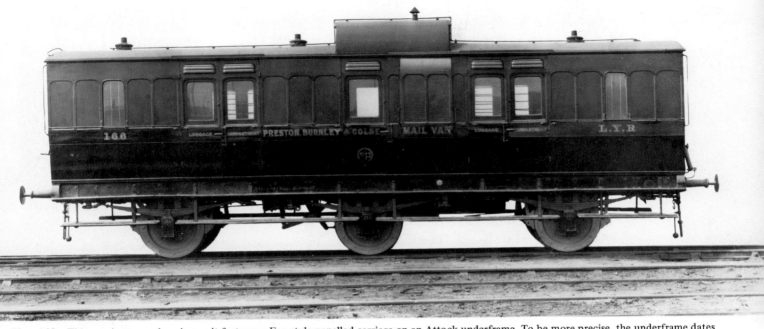

Plate 165　This van is an anachronism as it features a Fay style panelled carriage on an Attock underframe. To be more precise, the underframe dates from about 1890 and is of standard Attock design, but the body appears to be two Fay carriages pieced together to fit the underframe. From the left hand end to the 'N' in 'VAN' is one old four wheel body length and the remainder is two thirds of a similar brake vehicle. Hence the birdcage has become sandwiched in the centre. Windows have been barred, gas lighting installed and a stove fitted, the only one known in a non-passenger coaching stock L&Y vehicle and whose cowl must have been right on the limits of the loading gauge. By some quirk, the L&Y had become the only railway allowed by the postal authorities to forward mails by goods train but this seems to be the East Lancashire line's own passenger train vehicle and it illustrates the amazing lengths to which the L&Y could go in utilizing older stock.

National Railway Museum

Plate 166　The final development of horse-box on the L&Y was this 16 ft. 6 in. example built to Diagram 109A in 1901, and a total of seventy three were built up to 1919. Attock had introduced his standard design of horse-box in 1879 (Diagram 108), which was superseded by an improved design to similar dimensions in 1892 (Diagram 109). No. 158 is an enlarged version of Diagram 109 but the increase added only a few inches to the length and width. Oil axleboxes were fitted for the first time and the style featured 'curved sides' (i.e., a tumblehome). Horse-boxes were numbered in their own series within the non-passenger coaching stock. Internally, the groom's compartment was 6 ft. 0 in. wide and the horses had 9 ft. 6¾ in. There was a small sliding door about 15 in. square which allowed the groom to examine the horses in transit and there were three stalls in each vehicle. These horse-boxes were the first ones to have the enamelled cast iron mangers. Externally, the door and window fittings were those used on carriage stock of the period, but the horse-boxes never had the plywood overlay to smooth the sides as did the carriages, and the planks were always visible. Oil lighting was standard to the end, some lasting into BR days. The vehicles were fitted with vacuum, Westinghouse and handbrakes. As with all L&Y carriages and non-passenger coaching stock, Mansell wood disc wheels were used.

National Railway Museum

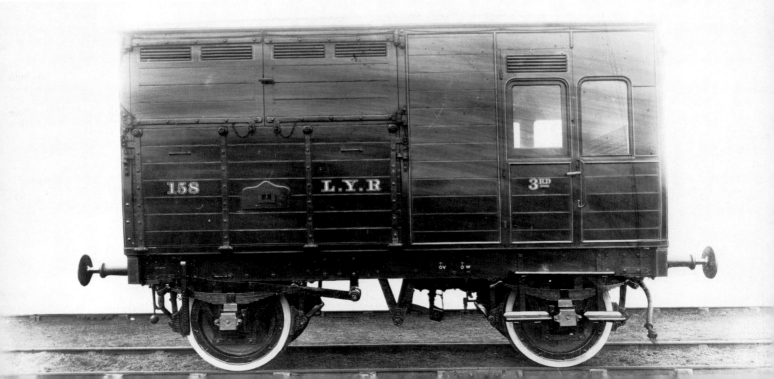

WAGONS AND GOODS YARDS

At its amalgamation with the LNWR on 1st January 1922, the L&Y owned around 38,000 wagons. A complete account taken on 31st December 1920 revealed 37,585 at an average cost of £83 0s 7d each, a total investment of over £3.1 million. There were 26,623 open merchandise, 7,259 covered goods, 1,721 coal and coke wagons, 714 cattle wagons, 340 ballast wagons and 928 brakes. Over 98 per cent of the stock was less than thirty years old and there was one wagon which had reached the ripe old age of 69. There were three major style periods of construction; up to 1901, the short 9 ft. 0 in. wheelbase vehicles from Fay and Attock's days; from 1902 to 1910, the large 12 ft. 0 in. wheelbase wagons, roughly from Banks' reign, and from 1910, until grouping, a medium sized 20 ft. 0 in. long vehicle on a 10 ft. 6 in. wheelbase, in the era of Gobey. The ensuing photographs are a random selection of wagon types before going on to look at goods yards and facilities.

Plate 167 (top) One of one hundred 20T coal wagons built to Order Y38 in 1907 and designed for coaling ocean-going steamers. However, in later years, such traffic declined and these half end door wagons, by now numbering three hundred, were often used on general merchandise or cotton traffic *(see Plate 180)*. The vehicle is typical of L&Y wagon policy and design for the middle period, 21 ft. 6 in. long, 8 ft. 0 in. wide, 12 ft. 0 in. wheelbase, a vacuum fitted steel underframe and height of 9 ft. 9 in. from rail to top of side.

National Railway Museum

Plate 169

Plate 170 (top) A close up view of the exterior details and internal ironwork arrangements on a 21ft. 6in. double end door wagon, built to Diagram 63. There were 1,310 examples built of this common L&Y type. This illustrates the general state that a wagon out in traffic would reach. The photograph is one of a series of Great War views of women at work and shows a routine examination of journals taking place on an oil axlebox. A private owner wagon, with individual corner ironwork pieces and round top end, is next in line.

B. C. Lane Collection

Plate 171 (middle) and 172 (bottom) The 20T all steel hopper was developed by the L&Y largely for its own use for gravity coal unloading at power stations such as Formby and Clifton, although Horwich and Newton Heath also had allocations. One hundred and thirty two were built, between 1904 and 1918, to Diagram 54, in five batches and of two different heights. Sixty six were 8ft. 6in. high and the same number was built to 9ft. 3in. height. They were 21ft. 0in. long, 8ft. 0in. wide and had a 12ft. 0in. wheelbase. *Plate 171* is an official view of one of the lower wagons whilst *Plate 172* is the internal view of a similar wagon giving an insight into its very different method of construction. The intriguing yard at Newton Heath Carriage & Wagon Works is seen at the rear.

R. J. Essery Collection and National Railway Museum

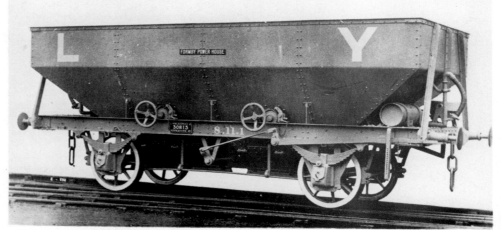

Plates 168 (left middle) and 169 (bottom) Two vans showing the final stages of L&Y covered goods design. *Plate 168* is one of six motor car vans built to Diagram 89 in 1913 as part of Order D49, which was for one hundred and thirty covered goods wagons, one hundred and twenty four of which were turned out to the almost identical Diagram 88. The major alteration was the provision of end doors for loading but the design does not seem to have been prepared very carefully, as the totally unecessary tarpaulin roof rollback has been retained. The large 'V' means vacuum fitted and was applied only to vans, as was the wagon running number on the sides and ends. At a cost of £131, these vehicles cost nearly £35 more than their standard counterparts. *Plate 169* shows virtually the ultimate development of covered goods design, for No. 38761 is the highest L&Y wagon running number which I have ever recorded. The vehicle was built to Diagram 99 and Order T58 in 1922 by Cravens of Sheffield. After the Great War, the Company turned to several outside wagon builders to provide new or replacement vehicles as its own shops were full. The wagon number is painted in a non-standard style, presumably by Cravens. A sister wagon survived until 1955 as No. M168760.

J. B. Hodgson Collection and H. N. Twells Collection

Plate 173   The art of wagon building is shown at its finest in this photograph of Refrigerator Van No. 37220, seen in works grey livery, which was turned out, in May 1914, to Order A51 and was destined to become the last new L&Y Refrigerator Van. The order was for twenty five vehicles and was the only Lot rated to carry 10T. They were built at a cost of £172 1s 1d each and were allocated to Diagram 48. They were 18 ft. 0 in. long, 7 ft. 6 in. wide and had a 10 ft. 0 in. wheelbase. Vacuum and Westinghouse brake cylinders and a train pipe were fitted, and these vans were almost non-passenger coaching stock. The usual livery incorporated a white body and solebars with black running gear and lettering exactly as shown in this photograph taken on 15th May 1914.

National Railway Museum

Plate 174   A twin timber wagon built to Diagram 36A. This wagon type was evolved in 1882, although the middle 1890s proved to be its most popular time when close on one hundred and seventy pairs were built, the last order being completed in 1896. Suddenly, in 1916, an order, Y53, was placed for forty more pairs and this picture shows part of that order. It was completed in 1917 at a cost of over £206 per pair, almost double that of 1896. The wagons were almost an anachronism, other railways having moved on to bogie bolsters. They were of a 6 ft. 0 in. wheelbase and the 14 ft. 0 in. individual wagon lengths made them 29 ft. 0 in. overall. Only the oil axleboxes and date '1/17' testify to their relative modernity. Almost equally incredible is that at least one pair survived until the mid-1950s being photographed with BR numbers.

National Railway Museum

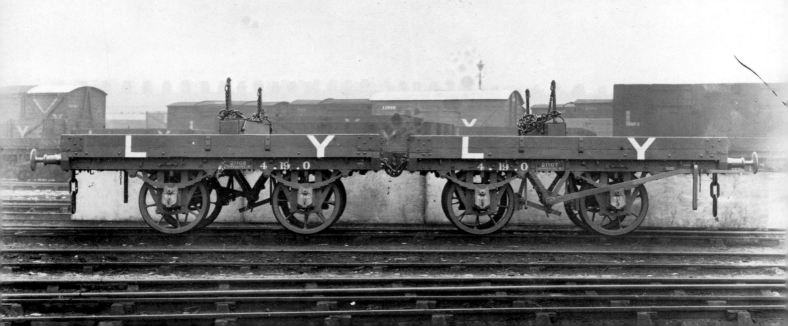

Plate 175 By contrast this massive Well Wagon was built in 1912, one of two to Order T46, for £305 14s 3d which made them the most expensive L&Y open goods wagons. Allocated to Diagram 87, it was 40 ft. 0 in. long, 31 ft. 0 in. between the bogies which were of 5 ft. 6 in. diamond frame type. Rail clearance was 8 in. and the well was 21 ft. 0 in. long. It was a multi-purpose type, taking up to 40 tons over the bolsters as the timber baulks, 25 tons across the solebars and 10 tons in the well itself. Potential loads would include industrial boilers and excessively large trees.

National Railway Museum

Plate 176 The photograph shows the standard L&Y 20T Loco Coal wagon, 21 ft. 6 in. long, 8 ft. 0 in. wide and with a 12 ft. 0 in. wheelbase, complete with shed allocation plate. This was one of a batch of one hundred built to Order D37 in 1906, with a specialized roller bearing axlebox known as 'Anti Friction Gear' costing an additional £20 on top of the usual £113 per wagon. Allocated Diagram 67, these wagons were the first to be 10 ft. 0 in. high from rail to top of side. The axlebox experiment was not perpetuated on subsequent orders.

National Railway Museum

Plate 177 For more than thirty yea
from the 1880s, this was the typic
L&Y Break Van. It was a total
enclosed ten tonner with sheet iron sid
on a wooden frame. Over five hundr
and twenty were built and gained t
nickname 'Tin Tabs' (Tin Tabernacle
They were 15 ft. 6 in. long, only 6
10 in. wide over the body but 7 ft. 10 i
over the footsteps and had a 9 ft. 0 i
wheelbase. They were allocated Diagra
21 and about three hundred and seven
five were still running in LMS da
although they suffered an early demi
on account of their low weight. 'Break
were allocated to goods depots or lar
yards and in earlier days, even
particular guards. No. 25100 was phot
graphed early in 1902 at Poulton. At th
stage most L&Y wagons carried t
'Illiterate' symbol of circle and triangl
instituted for those workers who cou
not read. The large letters did not arri
until 1905.

The late J. M. Tomlinso

Plate 178 Daisyfield Junction goods yard (Blackburn), looking towards Great Harwood and the outlet to the former East Lancashire line, in 1903. The photograph was taken to show the 40T Goliath travelling crane then recently installed. The stock on view is typical of the time showing almost universally open merchandise with many tarpaulins in evidence. Gas lamps, loading gauges, carts, loads and general clutter enhance the scene.

National Railway Museum

Plate 179   An interesting picture showing No. 33452 arriving at Newton Heath following extensive damage by fire in September 1921. It would appear that the wagon had been a 21 ft. 6 in. sliding door covered goods wagon built to Diagram 73. Underneath, is wagon No. 6093, an older example from Diagram 2 and uncommon because of its length. Even as late as this, this wagon carries only 'Illiterate' symbols and is now part of the stores department at Knottingley. In due course, a new No. 33452 will take the road with much of the ironwork visible in this picture being used again.

National Railway Museum

Plate 180   A scene inside one of the sheds at North Docks goods yard, Liverpool, on 24th November 1913, which displays the prodigious amounts of cotton carried by the railway. Generally, one plank open wagons were used but often, as here, many other types were pressed into service. In view are three 20T 'Goole half-end door' coal wagons *(Plate 167)*, double-end door and fixed-end half box wagons, a 30T bogie half box and a couple of old two plankers. All are lettered 'L' and 'Y'. An overhead travelling crane, from which a pair of slightly elongated 'No. 17 cotton dogs for American bales' are slung, is provided for the transfer of loads, the weight limit being 15 cwt.

National Railway Museum

Plate 181 The L&Y provided the greatest movement of fresh fish from the west coast port of Fleetwood, itself a railway development. In addition to special sheds, special vehicles were constructed. This photograph, taken in August 1910, shows one of these four hundred and forty five very light pastel green vans, (Diagram 72), about to be loaded. They were dual fitted and steam-piped for any passenger train work, and they were built with concrete floors 3in. thick on top of the normal wooden floor canted to 2in. by the central drain. Speed was necessary to prevent the fish decomposing and special trains were often run *(see Plate 27)*.

National Railway Museum

Plate 182 This photograph shows goods facilities at the opposite end of the spectrum from the one shown in *Plate 183*; a single siding for very small establishments, or even for one private owner such as the one shown at Stubley, between Portsmouth and Cornholme. This particular connection was removed before 1922 and the land now forms a small housing estate. Only local street names and an additional retaining wall testify to its former guise.

Author's Collection

Plate 183 (below) Part of North Docks goods yard on 21st October 1909 when the railway was close to its zenith. It appears to be in a state of chaos, with wagons everywhere and merchandise seemingly left unattended. This yard dealt largely with traffic leaving Liverpool. The white area, above the covered goods wagons, houses cattle pens, as this yard was also the point of entraining for Irish cattle bound for the slaughter house at Salford.

P. Gibb Collection

ON SHED

On the L&Y, there were thirty two numbered running sheds of widely varying sizes, and one sub-shed, although there had been others at different locations at earlier dates. The sheds were organized into sixteen districts, until 1919, when a reorganization reduced the number to eight. Most shed buildings dated from the 1880 to 1900 period when Barton Wright and his successors were expanding the provision of accommodation. The sheds were often the dead end type with an office block at one side. They were adequate for early twentieth century requirements and few piecemeal additions were made, thanks to the sound early planning.

Shed	Code	District	District after 1919	Notes
Newton Heath	1	Newton Heath	Newton Heath	
Low Moor	2	Low Moor	Low Moor	
Sowerby Bridge	3	Low Moor	Low Moor	
Leeds	4	Low Moor	Low Moor	
Mirfield	5	Mirfield	Low Moor	
Wakefield	6	Wakefield	Wakefield	
Normanton	7	Wakefield	Wakefield	
Barnsley	8	Wakefield	Wakefield	
Knottingley	9	Wakefield	Wakefield	Closed 1st July 1922
Goole	10	Goole	Wakefield	
Doncaster	11	Wakefield	Wakefield	Engines kept at GN shed
Hull	12	Agecroft	Newton Heath	
Agecroft	13	Agecroft	Newton Heath	Sub-shed York
Bolton	14	Bolton	Bolton	
Horwich	15	Bolton	Bolton	
Wigan	16	Wigan	Bolton	
Southport	17	Sandhills	Sandhills	
Sandhills (Bank Hall)	18	Sandhills	Sandhills	Renamed 1920
Aintree (Sorting Sidings)	19	Aintree	Sandhills	
Bury	20	Bury	Bury	
Bacup	21	Bacup	Bury	
Accrington	22	Accrington	Accrington	
Rose Grove	23	Accrington	Accrington	
Colne	24	Accrington	Accrington	
Lower Darwen	25	Lower Darwen	Accrington	
Hellifield	26	Lower Darwen	Accrington	
Lostock Hall	27	Lostock Hall	Blackpool	
Chorley	28	Bolton	Bolton	Closed 1st July 1922
Ormskirk	29	Aintree	Sandhills	
Fleetwood	30	Blackpool	Blackpool	
Blackpool (Talbot Road)	31	Blackpool	Blackpool	
Blackpool Central	32	Blackpool	Blackpool	

The ensuing photographs endeavour to show what happened on shed rather than displaying locomotives

Plate 184   The official photographer has captured the thrilling view that most shed visitors remember, as engines await their next duties at the doors of the shed. This is a fine view of Bolton, in May 1914, with two 4-4-0s and a 2-4-2T identifiable.

National Railway Museum

Plate 185

Plates 185 to 187 These pictures are part of a series of photographs taken at Bolton, in May 1914, which were used to instruct enginemen as to how to care for their locomotives. Such education was a tenet of Hughes who reckoned it would improve efficiency, increase availability of the engine and reduce repairs caused by bad enginemanship. *Plate 185* shows watering, with rebuilt 0-6-0, No. 1303 (Works No. 423 of 20th January 1896, rebuilt in November 1911, withdrawn in November 1934 as LMS No. 12325). *Plate 186* shows coaling with another Belpaire rebuild standing alongside and below, a line of loco coal wagons whence coal was shovelled into the tenders or bunkers. The gas lamp bracket was a standard feature, whilst the three plank wagon is a survivor from the early 1880s. Finally, *Plate 187* shows cleaning, with as much emphasis on safety as on instruction (the L&Y being quite safety conscious as their staff booklets show). No. 73 was built on 19th November 1894 and withdrawn, without alteration, as No. 12264 on 18th August 1934. *Plate 71* is also part of this series of photographs.

National Railway Museum

Plate 186

Plate 187

Plates 188 and 189   Lodging houses for enginemen were provided at the largest sheds, after the railway unions had won their battles over hours of working, and the photographs show the exterior and interior of the new accommodation at Wakefield on 12th July 1910. Somewhat barrack-like, perhaps expectedly, the interior shows the spartan dining room with its walls adorned with official locomotive pictures. The much smaller Blackpool lodging house still stands (1982), although it is no longer connected with railways.

National Railway Museum

Plate 190 (above)   Wheel drops, for examination or repairs, were installed at eight sheds. This view at Bolton, with safety boards removed, shows how the device operated. This picture was taken on 4th July 1910 and gives a goods view of the shed interior.

National Railway Museum

Plate 191 (left)   The assistant foreman's office at Aintree (Sorting Sidings) was a hut in the centre of the shed yard. The stove looks capable of creating a good 'fug' and the kettle a good brew, but the two telephones, switchboard and electric light testify as to the importance of the place. The message system for enginemen booking on and off is of great interest. Again locomotive photographs adorn the walls in this picture taken in August 1918.

National Railway Museum

Plates 192 (top right) and 193 (bottom right)   During the dry summers of 1910 to 1913, obtaining water at Blackpool Central shed became quite a problem as the shed supply was restricted by the town water board, its only source. However, Talbot Road had its own well and tenders were gathered together, filled and trundled round via Poulton and Wrea Green to Blackpool Central. *Plate 192* shows 0-6-0 No. 1030, (built February 1890, and eventually one of the last withdrawn in September 1962 as No. 52093), about to set off with such a mission. The headlamps are for a 'Class A' Fast Merchandise train, whilst it must be noted that, despite similar appearance, the first four tenders are all different in some way. *Plate 193*, shows the various contraptions and devices evolved to transfer and conserve water in the Blackpool district; a marvellous concoction of troughing and point lever! The locomotive is 0-6-0, No. 99 which was built in August 1906, rebuilt in November 1912 with the Belpaire boiler shown, and withdrawn in November 1960 as No. 52445. Both pictures were taken on 27th September 1913.

National Railway Museum

SHIPPING

The L&Y had two shipping fleets, one for the Irish Sea for traffic to the Isle of Man and Ireland, and one for the North Sea for Continental traffic. At the Grouping, the Company owned twenty eight ships and had a share in seven others, more than any other British railway. The separate fleets were identified by differently painted funnels and different flags at the mast-head. *Plate 306* shows the flag flown by the North Sea vessels in more detail.

Plate 194 *Mellifont*, a twin screw vessel, built by Vickers of Barrow in 1903, a gross tonnage of 1,204, was used on the Liverpool to Dublin (Drogheda) service, and is pictured here, in the Mersey, in 1905, probably just before transfer to the East Coast Fleet. She returned to the Drogheda run in 1912 and was withdrawn in 1933 after spending five years working from Holyhead to Dublin.

National Railway Museum

Plate 195 In 1905, the L&Y obtained the Goole Steam Shipping Company and opened up access to nine continental ports from Dunkirk to Hamburg. The docks at Goole were not railway property, but they were surrounded by railways. The New Dock (No. 5) is pictured here, from the deck of an unknown L&Y ship, looking towards the 50T crane. Across Stanhope Street beyond the *Wreathier* are the L&Y offices.

National Railway Museum

Plate 196 (above) The paddle steamer *Iverna* was built by A. & J. Inglis in 1895 for the Drogheda Steam Packet Company. This steamer became L&Y property on 22nd July 1902. A yellow band was added to the black funnel and she carried the red flag with the white letters 'L' and 'Y' and Company coat of arms; the flag of the Dublin run. Photographed on 21st June 1910, the *Iverna*, of 995 gross tonnage, was withdrawn in July 1912.

National Railway Museum

Plate 197 The sumptuous dining room of the *Duke of Cornwall*, a twin screw ship built by Vickers of Barrow in 1898 (of 1,540 gross tonnage). The ship was one of five built for the Fleetwood to Belfast service of the North Lancashire Steam Navigation Company which was jointly owned with the LNWR. The Belfast service, coupled with boat trains from London (LNWR), Leeds and Manchester *(see Plate 150)*, was one of the most prestigious on the L&Y.

National Railway Museum

Plate 198 Fleetwood is a classic example of railway enterprise in that, like Crewe, it was created by the railway. The docks at Fleetwood were all railway owned. The complex was designed by Sir John Hawkshaw for direct transhipment and no cartage. Construction was commenced by the Preston & Wyre Railway but completed by the L&Y. The *Rossall*, pictured here, was a P&WR twin screw ship of 1881 but only grossed 192 tons. Although tied up at the fish shed, she is used for general cargo, fish traffic being another enterprise exploited by the L&Y, *(see Plates 27 and 181)*. Photographed in 1910, this ship was disposed of in May 1913.

National Railway Museum

HORWICH WORKS

Another triumph for the L&Y was the new locomotive works at Horwich. It was Barton Wright, yet again, who placed before the Board of Directors the need for a new works. The Miles Platting Works was old, a hotchpotch of buildings, difficult to modernize and just not suitable for the sort of railway that Barton Wright had in mind. A list of requirements was drawn up, which included cheap level ground centrally located in close proximity to the system, with room for expansion. Various locations, such as Great Harwood, Moston and Brighouse, were studied, but in May 1884, the Board heard of a 650 acre estate for sale near Bolton, and Elias Dorning was despatched to the Mitre Hotel to try and secure the purchase for the L&Y. He was allowed to bid up to £65,000 at the auction. Dorning bought the lot for £36,000. The railway then sold off the chief rents on 200 acres of the estate and recouped not only the land costs, but also much of the building costs. Therefore the Company acquired its new works for almost nothing and, in so doing, spawned another railway town, as Horwich, as the area was known, had no engineering history whatsoever. In fact, men had to be brought in from Miles Platting and Bury to develop the works. Construction started in March 1885, workshops were completed in 1887 and No. 1008 rolled out on 20th February 1889. Superbly equipped and laid out, little alteration has had to take place over the past one hundred years and, after building over two thousand locomotives of all types, and repairing fifty thousand others, the works still has a future as part of British Rail Engineering Ltd.

The works was vast and the following photographs are meant to portray the flavour of life at the works, rather than record the engines which passed through. *See also Plates 288 and 289.*

▷

Plate 199 Two photographs showing a panorama across the west end of the works, depicting, from left to right, the office block, main stores, main check lodge (behind the wagons), paint shop, engine shed and No. 1 erecting shop. They were photographed on 17th July 1907.

National Railway Museum

Plate 200 Old engines seemed to congregate within Horwich Works. This particular one, No. 518 is an East & West Junction Railway order bought up cheaply by the L&Y and adapted for use as a crane tank. The front buffer beam was made of lead to counterbalance the crane and the engine sported a green livery for many years beyond the last green Barton Wright engine. It was probably the only L&Y locomotive working in the 20th century never to have a cast number-plate fitted, the only number being painted on the rear of the bunker. As the crane was rarely used, the engine spent much of its life wandering up and down with the 'Materials Cab', a small goods vehicle for conveying stores. It only accrued a small mileage and disappeared late in 1922.

B. C. Lane Collection

Plate 201 An 18in. gauge railway system was laid within the works for transporting materials and diminutive locomotives ordered for it. *Dot* was the first of three from Beyer Peacock in 1887, (Works No. 2823), and five more were later built at Horwich. They were all named after small objects, mostly insects, and carried the goods double red lining livery with a special small coat of arms. Two of these locomotives have been preserved.

B. H. Ellston Collection

Plate 202 (below) Electricity was provided on site at an early stage, and this photograph shows, on 11th April 1908, the electric crane provided at the rear of the stores.

National Railway Museum

Plate 203   The boiler shop and nearby store yard, photographed from the roof of the offices, on 27th July 1907. The trucks for moving boilers about are mostly the tender frames from Yates 2-4-0s, *(see Plate 40)*, with the centre wheels removed. The general orderliness can be appreciated.

National Railway Museum

Plate 204   Within the works, Barton Wright decided to incorporate a signal shop to build locking frames for signal cabins and thereby alleviate the need for contracts with outsiders. In many ways, the patterns of the Railway Signalling Company were used. Frames were built in banks of four levers although there was the provision to add an extra lever at the side of a bank if necessary. These frames were then shipped to site and the box was built around them. This twenty four lever bank was photographed in August 1919.

National Railway Museum

Plate 205 This scene shows the pits and specialized machinery installed in the boiler shop for hydraulic rivetting. Photographed in August 1919, it shows the 18 in. gauge railway inside the shop together with the youth of recruits.

National Railway Museum

Plate 206 In late 1904, Hughes devised an electrical fan, or blower, to help raise steam in cold engines. The idea was successful, reducing the time from two and a half hours to forty minutes, but it required block and tackle to move it, and a far greater time to fit and undo the device than was economical. The idea was therefore abandoned. An Aspinall 0-6-0 goods locomotive tries out the equipment on a damp 8th March 1905.

National Railway Museum

Plate 207 The L & Y was very safety conscious and, in the absence of good local authority fire fighting services, they maintained two trains in constant readiness, at Horwich and Newton Heath, to be despatched to the scene of any railway or adjacent fire. Practices at sheds or stations were frequent and annual competitions were held. This photograph shows the Horwich Brigade at practice, around December 1915, in the works yard. The train consists of the engine on duty on that day, 2-4-2T, No. 733, with a new (1914) purpose built 4,740 gallon water tank wagon No. 37068, the special Fire Brigade Van with pumping engine and, inevitably, a converted six wheeler in which the men would ride. With slight stock alterations, this train lasted until 1951.

National Railway Museum

ELECTRIFICATION

It was Sir John Aspinall who became very interested in the electrification of railways, largely as a result of his travels abroad. In it he saw the most favourable economic factors for the future after the initial capital outlay and several studies were prepared. The L&Y eventually decided upon third rail, rather than overhead electrification although, as the ensuing photographs show, the latter was also experimented with. From 1902 to 1918, much knowledge was gained and thoroughly reliable and quick services ensued bringing passengers back to the railway. Aspinall's theories would seem to have been vindicated.

Plates 208 and 209 The L&Y chose the Liverpool to Southport line for the first electrified installation, largely on grounds of convenience, and Dick Kerr, of Preston, received the contract for the electrical equipment. It was opened completely, with new electric cars in the usual passenger livery, on 13th May 1904, after minor teething troubles. The generous loading gauge allowed for 10 ft. 0 in. wide bodies on the American-looking 80 seat vehicles. *Plate 208* shows one of the trains at Southport, soon after introduction, with the usual formation of two 1st Class trailers flanked by two motor 3rds. The small '6' board was the train roster for the day. *Plate 209* is a later view, taken on 31st October 1911, of car No. 3037, a motor 3rd of 1906, which was soon rebuilt to the flat face front end seen in the picture. Bogies, current collection and methods of construction can all be viewed in this scene photographed in the sidings near Chapel Street Station, Southport. One of Barton Wright's 0-4-4T locomotives, used for carriage warming duties, stands in the background.

P. Gibb Collection and National Railway Museum

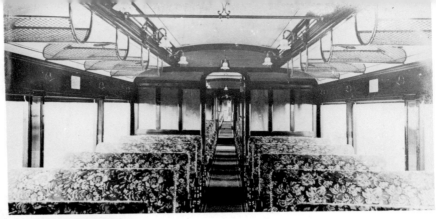

Plates 210 and 211 Two interiors, at different periods, of the Liverpool to Southport stock. *Plate 210* shows a July 1920 view of a 3rd Class open, externally similar to that shown in *Plate 209*. The map shows the full extent of the electrified lines in the area, although Ormskirk was not reached until 1913. The seating was rattan with oak finish, some seats were reversible, and the double swing doors separated the 'smoking' and 'non-smoking' sections. *Plate 211* is an early view of a 1st Class interior. The woodwork is mahogany with lighter panels and the flower weave upholstery was red and yellow in the 'smoking' and blue and yellow in the 'non-smoking' sections.

National Railway Museum and
A. G. Ellis Collection

Plate 212 The L&Y adopted 650 volts d.c. for this first electrification together with a fourth rail for the return of the current. The rail carrying the current was protected by a piece of wood either side, leaving the top open to the boot of a careless ganger. The proliferation of 'bits' at a junction caused the railway to look extremely untidy. This is the Station Junction at Aintree, Sefton Arms, on 21st February 1907. Kirkdale is ahead and Linacre Road to the right. The signal box in the distance was Aintree East on the line into Fazakerley Sidings.

National Railway Museum

Plate 213

Plates 213 and 214 The L&Y had ideas of electrifying the Manchester to Leeds main line, and experiments began with overhead current collection in 1912. Aintree Sorting Sidings was the chosen location and a set of 2-4-2 radial tank frames were used to make the first locomotive which used jackshaft drive and centre cab. Provision for overhead and third rail collection, both at 650 volts d.c., was made and the locomotive, numbered 1, became nicknamed *The Beetle (see Plate 214)*. It was supposed to work between Aintree Sorting Sidings and North Mersey goods, but it was not very successful and disappeared around 1914. The equipment used, *(see Plate 213)*, does not seem to have been too effective, with telegraph poles being used for the catenary supports, and the problems encountered, plus the onset of the Great War, turned the L&Y back toward third rail. The goods vehicles, train make up and yard furniture are of great interest in these two photographs.

National Railway Museum

Plate 214

Plate 215

Plates 216 (left above) and 217 (right above) 'Before and after' pictures show interior views of the 1916 Manchester to Bury stock. Apart from a wooden channel for the cable beneath the floor, these cars were of an all metal construction. *Plate 217* shows the use of rattan seating again in the 3rd Class. A great deal of the frills found on the Liverpool stock disappeared but these were constructed in wartime.

National Railway Museum

Plate 218 (below)   For the Manchester to Bury line, a return to third rail current collection was made, but this time 1,200 volts d.c. was chosen. This necessitated covering the live rail and current was thus collected from the side of the rail. Again, a fourth return rail was used but this was a much smaller square section and it had been tried previously on the Holcombe Brook branch. Operation commenced on 7th April 1916 with the new elliptical roof coaches shown. The usual five coach formation was motor-trailer-motor-trailer-motor, of which one trailer was 1st Class. Ninety three seats were to be found in 3rd Class trailers. Superbly finished and painted in the usual carriage livery, these cars contained all the knowledge which the L&Y had gained concerning electric railway working, but there were also some new ideas such as the buffer pads and the buckeye couplings. The system was considered the first part of an extensive Manchester urban electrification but these cars actually became the zenith of the L&Y and they were to work on for fully forty years.

J. B. Hodgson Collection

Plate 215 (left) In 1913, Messrs. Dick Kerr & Company approached the L&Y with a request to carry out an experimental electrification scheme, featuring 3,500 volts d.c. overhead collection, as they were interested in a contract in South America. Aspinall readily agreed, as they had had an excellent relationship when Dick Kerr & Company had worked on the Liverpool to Southport line, and Aspinall offered the Bury to Holcombe Brook line, a distance of 3¾ miles. Two motor and two trailer cars, all 3rd Class, were built by the L&Y, and are interesting design forerunners of the Manchester to Bury stock. The service began on 12th July 1913, all the electrical equipment being supplied by Dick Kerr & Company, and the photograph shows the more advanced thinking which was employed. This was the way to go in the future and only worries about difficulties at Manchester Victoria caused a reversion to third rail. In this photograph, motor car No. 3501 and trailer No. 3601 pass Bury South on an experimental training run on 27th June 1913. The successful system was removed in 1917 and replaced by the standard Manchester to Bury 1,200 volt d.c. third rail.

National Railway Museum

Plate 219 This motor 3rd has suffered in a small mishap and given us the opportunity to view the switchgear in the high tension compartment. As can be seen, all vehicle ends carried the destination blind and featured a driver's compartment enabling sets to be broken and reassembled at will. The additional dumb buffers are merely to shunt the car in the works. Pictured on 10th July 1917, an older wooden carriage, with a fixed gas lamp, on the next track is seen as a comparison.

National Railway Museum

Plate 220 (above) One of the two baggage cars built for the Liverpool to Southport service. The photograph features a very different style of construction from the service stock in addition to the odd bogies, only one of which was powered. This particular vehicle was badly damaged in an air raid on Liverpool Exchange in May 1941 and was withdrawn soon after as LMS No. 28497. It was 54 ft. 0 in. long but only 8 ft. 9 in. wide. There was a 34 ft. 2 in. luggage compartment and a 9 ft. 6 in. workmen's compartment with bench seating. There was also a motorman's compartment at each end and all doors were hinged.

National Railway Museum

Plate 221 (below) This device, yet another old six wheel carriage, was prepared in 1917 as an attempt to keep the conductor rails clean. The internal arrangements featured a small oil-fired steam engine, pipework to blow steam on the rails and signal levers to operate the wire brushes. The vehicle worked at night, or on Sundays, when the electric service was less frequent.

National Railway Museum

Plate 222 (top left)   Special uniforms were provided for motormen, incorporating a plain single breasted jacket buttoned to the neck. However, in the summer of 1917, a new style was prepared featuring breast and side pockets and exposing the necktie. Here are three of the Sandhills motormen displaying the old and new uniforms on 28th July 1917.

National Railway Museum

Plate 223 (top right)   The motorman's driving position on the Liverpool to Southport stock, as viewed through the door into the driving compartment. Photographed on 31st October 1911, this car has the flat face front end.

National Railway Museum

Plate 224 (left)   In order to warn the general public of the extra danger near electric lines, special notices were cast and placed close to the normal trespass notices. This notice was photographed at Crossens on 12th March 1912, and is also shown in *Plate 102*.

National Railway Museum

Plate 225 (below)   With domestic electricity supply in its infancy, the L&Y was forced to provide its own current from its own power stations. For the Liverpool to Southport line, Formby, with several boosters, was the generating station, whilst the Manchester to Bury power station was at Clifton Junction. Surprisingly, this power station was two miles, as the crow flies, from the nearest electric rail, but it was the best site. The power station commenced operations in 1914 and closed in 1933, whereafter power came from the National Grid. The brickwork style is reminiscent of Horwich and Newton Heath Works. For many years a small battery operated electric locomotive shunted the coal and ash wagons in and out of the power station. The photograph shows Clifton Junction in 1915.

National Railway Museum

The L&Y attempted many experiments during its existence, many of them in the interests of economy. These efforts were sometimes to be seen by the travelling public. However, this was not always the case nor was the education of the workforce neglected. All this was in the interests of efficiency. The Company was not termed 'The Business Line' without reason.

Plate 226 A view of part of the Signalling School established at Manchester Victoria in 1910. Its main aim was to teach aspiring signalmen the mechanics of their block instruments and levers and how to work them. A model, slightly larger than 'O' gauge, was built by Horwich apprentices to help demonstrate how things worked. The model is still in use (1982) and great attention to detail is taken, no train moving without the appropriate signalling first taking place. In addition to the model and its L&Y stock there was also a full size lever frame and various standard signals which have now been replaced by more modern equipment over the years. At the school, in L&Y days, many other subjects were dealt with for the benefit of all types of staff.

National Railway Museum

Plate 227 Another innovation was train control. This developed slowly, arising from the need to prevent excessive congestion and it commenced, with the organization of all goods trains and goods wagons, in August 1915. Offices at Manchester Victoria, which were continuously manned, were equipped with telephones, board maps and a card system for controlling the whereabouts of all trains. These whereabouts had to be notified to the controllers. There were four main areas and three other centres for localized freight working. This board shows the Liverpool, or Western Area, the line down the centre is a window reflection. The original is clear enough to read even small sidings, and the lettering seems to have been done by one of the signwriters employed on the goods stock (his 'Rs' are unmistakable, *(see Plate 173)*.

National Railway Museum

Plates 228 and 229   By 1921, the power limitations of the Hughes railmotors were already apparent and a new means had to be devised to provide greater flexibility of stock, increased passenger accommodation and simplification of station movements wherever possible. One answer to this was the 'Reversible Train'. A 2-4-2T was modified to allow the driver to drive from the guard's end when necessary, and two normal corridor coaches were attached, one of which had larger windows at the guard's end to permit the driver to see the road ahead. *Plate 228* shows that it was essentially a push-pull unit. Power for the driver's linkages came from a Westinghouse pump and *Plate 229* shows the modified cab on a 2-4-2T and was photographed in March 1922.

National Railway Museum

ROAD VEHICLES

In the L&Y accounting system, road vehicles were split into two types. Parcels and luggage on carts and on vans was charged to the carriage accounts, whilst goods on floats, drays and lurries were part of the goods stock accounts. Since the traffic emanated from different sources and travelled in different trains, the policy is understandable. The ensuing photographs show some of the variety of vehicles which could be found.

Plates 230 to 233   Four types of hand-drawn carts or trolleys in common use. *Plate 230* shows the No. 1 type four wheel platform truck fitted with a high cage and featuring dropsides. The split spoke wheels were a distinctive L&Y feature. *Plate 231* is the No. 2 type platform truck with an unusual wheel arrangement. *Plate 232* is a 'Three-Quarter Truck' for large sacks and *Plate 233* is a No. 2 handcart, probably similar to the type used by Outdoor Porter Winch *(Plate 2)*. Details on this type have survived showing that the wheels were 3 ft. 0 in. in diameter and the cart was 5 ft. 0 in. long and 2 ft. 6 in. wide. The ends and tapered sides were detachable. The cost of each cart was £6 8s 3d and it weighed 1¾ cwt.

H. N. Twells Collection and J. B. Hodgson Collection

Plate 230

Plate 231

Plate 232

Plate 233

Plate 234 One of sixteen two wheel parcel carts which could carry 15 cwt. It weighed half a ton, could hold 90 cu. ft. of goods and cost £51 to build. It was painted in carriage livery with a brown and cream interior.

J. B. Hodgson Collection

Plate 235 An older, medium sized, four wheel parcel cart, with a carrying capacity of 25 cwt. in 126 cu. ft. of space. The design of this particular vehicle seems to have been influenced by Fay and it has been hand lettered. It must have been something of a period piece even when photographed around 1920.

J. B. Hodgson Collection

Plate 236 One of the commonest L&Y delivery vehicles, the 30 cwt. parcel dray, was a 2 plank open dray with a lettered tarpaulin cover on a wire frame. There were sixty four such vehicles and a similar example has been preserved in the National collection. They were painted in the carriage dark brown livery and had the legend, 'Lancashire & Yorkshire Railway Company, Victoria Station XXX' (the dray number being XXX) on the bottom rail. These carts were charged to passenger stock and each cost approximately £42 15s 6d. Above the drays in this picture is a delightful scalloped effect to the canopy.

J. B. Hodgson Collection

Plates 237 to 239 A set of three photographs, taken in July 1921, at Bridge Street goods yard, Bradford to show the advantages of motor haulage and at the same time displaying L&Y carting practises. *Plate 237* is a standard horse-drawn 30 cwt. lurry with twenty bales of wool stacked on a separate pallet. The L&Y organized their loads into pallets to minimise turn round time at goods depots which enabled an already loaded pallet to be quickly swung into place. The loading gauges seen on the goods shed behind are lettered 'L&Y'. *Plate 238* shows Sentinel steam waggon Regn. No. AW 8589, which was road motor No. 129 also carrying twenty bales of wool but which has no pallet. These vehicles were painted in the carriage purple brown livery with cream letters and blue shading, even though they were classed as goods stock. *Plate 239* shows the final development to the petrol-engined lorry, a Karrier (of Huddersfield) chassis, Regn. No. NB 9644, with Newton Heath body and cab, carrying ten sacks of stuffing. The speed restriction was 12 m.p.h., but this was still well in excess of the horse. The front mudguard has a tracery all its own. Bradford Bridge Street also featured a horse hospital for the Percherons, the dray horses which the L&Y preferred to use, their feet being better suited to the stone setts encountered.

National Railway Museum

Plate 237

Plate 238

Plate 239

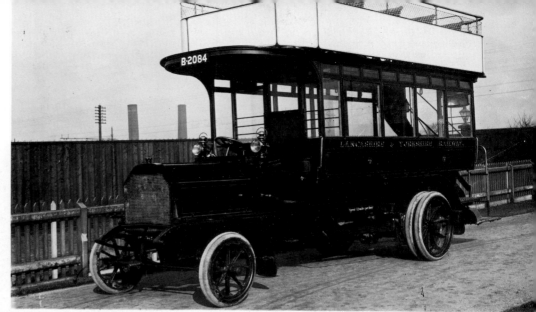

Plates 240 and 241 The L&Y ventured into motor omnibuses almost as soon as they became viable, this being dictated by the competition from the electric tramcars. Two Milnes-Daimler chassis were obtained and bodies were placed upon them at Newton Heath. *Plate 240* shows the first bus at Horwich on 27th February 1907. Initially two routes were covered, one around Crosby and the other from Chorley to Bamber Bridge. Regn. No. B 2084 was later withdrawn and replaced by a Commer, Regn. No. B 2156. In 1910 Regn. No. B 2084 was converted to a lorry, thereby becoming the first of that motor fleet *(Plate 241)*. With a carrying capacity of only 2½ tons, its days were numbered and it was withdrawn in 1920. In due course both bus services were withdrawn and the vehicles were scrapped.

National Railway Museum

Plate 242 An experiment in palletisation and transference seen at Blackburn on 5th April 1920. The pallet, or 'flat bottom' as it was termed, was to be winched away from the lurry to the motor lorry in a complicated looking way and the object of the exercise, either to speed loading or unloading, has been lost in the mists of time. The motor lorry is No. 18, Regn. No. NA 5365.

National Railway Museum

Plate 243 (above) A corner of Newton Heath Works, on 10th December 1919, where a large number of ex-Great War vehicles are undergoing rebuilding, repainting and eventual re-registration. They stand alongside some of the wagon stock. The majority seen here are Leylands which had already spent some time on the road on deliveries and the method of building the standard L&Y motor lorry cab is on view, to the left of No. 95. Other fleet vehicles to be seen are Nos. 15, 21 and 45.

National Railway Museum

Plates 244 (middle) and 245 (bottom) The final versions of two L&Y motor lorries. No. 42 is an ex-Great War refurbished Leyland used for goods deliveries, and as rugged as they come, whilst *Plate 245* shows No. 189, a Ford open type built to carry 15 cwt. of parcels and commissioned in July 1921 after costing £285. Pneumatic tyres and electric headlamps are features of this all new post-war era vehicle.

B. C. Lane Collection and J. B. Hodgson Collection

SIGNALS AND SIGNAL CABINS

Initially the L&Y used outside contractors for their signalling with the Railway Signalling Company holding the contract when Horwich Works was opened. In 1891 the company took the decision to make their own equipment and a separate signal shop was created at Horwich (see Plate 204), H. Raynar Wilson being appointed Signal Engineer. Many of the designs of the RSC were adopted, standard length cabins were designed and, even as early as 1895, the L&Y was a well signalled railway. Over the 529 route miles then opened, there were over 600 signal boxes controlling 11,511 signals, which averaged out at 21.7 signals per mile. The Midland average was 9.7 and the GWR a lowly 5.0. These photographs show something of the developments over the years.

Plate 246   Like many railways, the L&Y began with disc, or bar and disc, signalling devices, but the intensity of traffic on the L&Y caused their early replacement. The one pictured here is reputed to be the last such device on the L&Y controlling a crossing near Blackrod and photographed shortly before its removal on 17th December 1907.

National Railway Museum

Plates 247 (below left) 248 (below right) and 249 (overleaf top)   Early signal cabins were often built on site to suit the situation, and one style which emerged, in the late 1870s and early 1880s, was this hip roof brick base design seen at Aspen Colliery (Plate 247). The style was later replaced by the standard brick base structure. An L&Y style ground signal is seen nearest the camera. Plate 248 shows a similar style hip roof cabin and this four storey elevated structure was a fairly common feature where road bridges impaired the view and where sighting was imperative. Massive timber shorting suggests that the cabin is a little unsteady. The original has an even taller home and distant signal in the background with the lovely RSC decorative post tops behind the arms. Plate 249 is 'something else'; a wooden lean-to structure with a charm all its own. It was renamed Wigan No. 3 in 1894 and was replaced in July 1941.

A. Wilkinson Collection and National Railway Museum

Plates 250 (below left) and 251 (below right)   The exterior and interior views of Kirkham North Junction box, a longer than usual standard, brick-base cabin. Although the frame was made at Horwich, its basic design came from the Railway Signalling Company. The box is as built and the levers were coloured red for home, green for distant, black for points and white for spare. Where necessary, brown was for use with level crossings. In building, use was made of standard signal parts wherever possible and suspended shelves held the block instruments. The cabins were well designed and many of the boxes featured upstairs 'privvies'.

A. G. Ellis Collection

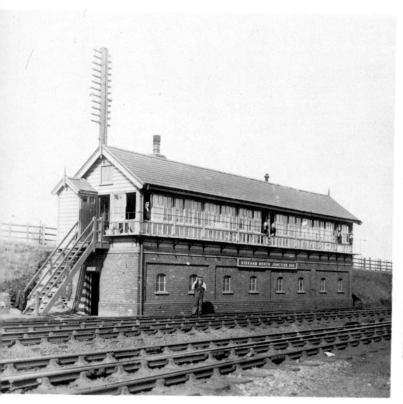

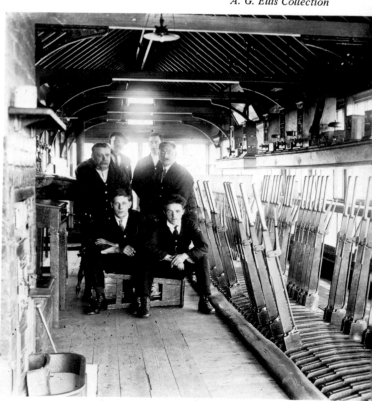

Plate 252 Whilst Atlantic No. 1395 heads, near Middleton Junction, for Manchester with an express from Leeds, the principle feature in this photograph is the double arm signal. The black base on the white post is 4 ft. above the ballast. The inspection platforms for each arm, connected by ladder, and the balance weights part way up the post are distinctive L&Y practices. Both arms are red, but the distant now has a chevron, a 1908 innovation. The steep angle of drop to the 'off' position is shown and these are the older style of arms fitted from 1891 to about 1910. They were 3 ft. 11¾ in. from pivot to board end and were designed by Raynar Wilson to replace the old single spectacle arms, *(see Plate 9,* gantry*)*, without needing to alter any other fittings. The older ball finial sits atop the post to protect the wood.

The late G. W. Smith

Plate 253 In restricted locations, a shorter arm was used, and on this post the much smaller shunting arm is to be seen, whilst the letter 'S' was not always used in such situations. Part of the bottleneck at Bradford Exchange can be seen, in this companion photograph to *Plate 109,* beneath the bridge.

National Railway Museum

Plate 254 In 1919, Southport Chapel Street was resignalled with an electro-pneumatic system and R. G. Berry was the man in charge. The new installation made little difference to the signals themselves, other than a lack of wiring, but this picture, taken near the station box, shows a newer type signal arm controlling the entry to the platforms from the Liverpool line. It was signal No. 20 on the board and the companion shunting signal, No. 19, is seen below it. In order to simplify matters, Berry and H. W. Moore designed a route indicator, here showing '2' for platform 2. There was a choice of three. Additional guying has been necessary to secure the signal. 'Rule 55 Exempt' discloses that track circuiting has been installed. The electric cars in the background and 3rd and 1st trailers and the scene was photographed in January 1920.

National Railway Museum

Plates 255 and 256 As a front runner in the development of signalling, the L&Y attempted some early electro-pneumatic schemes at busy locations. With the electrification and growing popularity as a seaside resort, a feasibility study, at Southport, revealed the need to extend to a fourth manual box, raising the number of levers to 340, but with electro-pneumatics, two boxes and 160 levers could perform the same work. *Plate 255* shows the station box which dates from 1917 and was peculiar in that it reintroduced the hip roof. All round visibility was a necessity with lines and engines arriving from several directions. Power was supplied from a separate power house. The interior *(Plate 256)*, was a strange layout in its day, with a bank of 87 stub levers, rising from a wooden cabinet, 68 of which were operable.

continued from above

The relays and interlocks filled the underneath of the cabinet and were visible from the other side. Of the many interesting features, the best are the megaphone, the fire extinguisher (with Company crest), the pneumatic gauge, electric light, and the apparent reduction in block instrument sizes. The mid position of some levers arises from their control of signals at facing junctions, where one lever could control two signals and yet keep both 'on'.

National Railway Museum

Plate 257 One of the reasons for the choice of electro-pneumatics, was the proximity of the live electric rails which took up much of the space required by manual rodding. Here the cover has been removed to show how it all works, in a photograph taken specifically for an information and publicity booklet. With this installation, not only points and signals were controlled, but the track was also circuited resulting in one of the first occasions when continuous displays of the whereabouts of trains could be seen. Over on platform 4, is 'open' 3rd No. 3301, the interior style of which was to become accepted throughout Britain by BR days.

National Railway Museum

Plate 258   A standard all wood signal box, with decorative barge boarding, at Aintree Sorting Sidings. The L & Y used the terms 'Box' and 'Cabin' indiscriminately. Much interesting yard furniture can be seen in this photograph, taken on 25th September 1912, and some of the overhead wiring is on display *(see also Plates 213 and 214)*.

National Railway Museum

Plate 259   The gorgeous array of signalling which greeted arrivals to Blackpool Central, before the Moore & Berry route indicators were installed. Of this view, taken in May 1921, only the Tower and a few buildings to the right remain today. However, this scene is, somehow, the epitome of Blackpool and day trips to the seaside. It remains one of my personal favourites. All the arms are of the older Raynar Wilson type.

National Railway Museum

ACCIDENTS

The L&Y seemed to experience more than its fair share of relatively gruesome accidents involving loss of life, but then you have to take into account the intensity of service which it operated. It was every bit as safe as, and probably more safety conscious than, many other railways, large and small.

Plate 260 The derailment of 2-4-2T, No. 670, and its train at Waterloo on 1st July 1903, was caused by the failure of the right trailing coupled wheel spring buckle. The engine left the rails at 50 m.p.h. and reduced parts of the station to matchwood. There were seven fatalities and a considerable amount of clearing up had already taken place by the time this photograph was taken.

P. Gibb Collection

Plate 261 The unfortunate result of the Hall Road collision of 27th July 1905. A Liverpool to Southport express was turned into the empty stock siding at that station and crashed, with much force, into the back of a recently cleared train, causing twenty one deaths and injuries to forty five persons. This photograph shows the front bogie of the electric car pushed back beyond the centre line. The other pair do not belong to this car but are the remains of the last carriage of the empty stock train. The force of the collision pushed the bogies to their respective positions and destroyed all trace of the upper parts. As a result of a public outcry, after the accident, a general revision of electric train working followed.

P. Gibb Collection

Plate 262 The unfortunate engine, pictured here, is a large boiler 0-8-0, No. 1365, which overran the signals, on Wednesday, 4th January 1922, at the end of the loop line opposite Mirfield No. 5 cabin, early in 'Division B' days. The driver, A. Avison, and fireman, M. Marshall, were not the first to come to grief here, as a Ramsbottom DX 0-6-0 was similarly deposited in March 1895. The 0-8-0 was lifted on 8th January and, prior to removal, presented a nice view of a tender top.

R. Stansfield Collection

Plates 263 and 264 Two views of the wreckage following the Charlestown Curve accident near Hebden Bridge on 21st June 1912, when a 2-4-2T, No. 276, severely spread the track whilst negotiating the reverse curves at speed. The engine and carriages overturned and the train dragged along for many yards. The express was the 2.25 p.m. Manchester to Leeds, and several lives were lost. As ever, a large crowd of interested onlookers have gathered. These powerful 2-4-2Ts were found to be too heavy and badly balanced for express work, and were transferred to the East Lancashire to Manchester locals where some of their power could be economically used on the steep gradients.

T. Wray Collection

Plate 264

Plate 265 Penistone Viaduct, several months after the collapse of one of the arches, displaying an interesting view of its interior construction. The accident occurred on 2nd February 1916, when the second and third arches gave way beneath 2-4-2T, No. 661. After being suspended on the rails for a few seconds, the engine then plunged 85 ft. into the valley below. Many photographs of the engine have been published but not many of the viaduct. In due course, both engine and viaduct were repaired and restored.

J. B. Hodgson Collection

Plate 266 This picture of carriage No. 2270, which was damaged in an accident at Dobbs Brow on 21st April 1921, provides greater insight into the principles of L&Y carriage construction. The carriage is an eight compartment all 3rd non-corridor on 6 ft. 6 in. bogies.

National Railway Museum

Plate 267 The 30T crane, bought from Cowan Sheldon, Carlisle in 1906 (Works No. 2954) and which was, for five years, the largest on the L&Y. It received the running number 2265 and was matched with wagon No. 32314 (built to drawing 6203 and Order K40). The crane base was 27 ft. 0 in. long, 8 ft. 6½ in. wide and 13 ft. 0 in. from rail to top of cab. The match wagon was 19 ft. 0 in. long on a 10 ft. 0 in. wheel-base and was vacuum fitted. The crane was first allocated to Sandhills, and in January 1912, it was transferred to Wakefield. It was loaned to the Government during the Great War, from 1916 to 'demobbing' in 1920. In LMS days, it went to Leeds in 1925 and down to Sheffield Grimesthorpe in 1931 where it was renumbered RS 1019/30. It was withdrawn in 1968. During L&Y days it attended many accidents including Charlestown Curve and it can just be identified in *Plate 263*.

National Railway Museum

Plate 268 This complete breakdown train was allocated to Newton Heath about 1914. It comprised, from the tender, travelling van No. 11, a 32 ft. 0 in. six wheel former passenger brake; match wagon No. 30456, a 21 ft. 6 in. long vehicle with a 12 ft. 0 in. wheelbase and vacuum fitted; 25T steam crane No. 2231, (Cowan Sheldon Works No. 2545 of 1902); packing wagon No. 9777, a very old adapted low goods wagon with through pipe and tool van No. 159, another 32 ft. 0 in. ex-passenger brake. The crane had a very varied career, being moved to Plaistow in March 1931, renumbered RS 1062/20 in 1941, transferred to Gloucester in August 1942 and eventually was withdrawn in 1971. The locomotive is No. 102, (Works No. 732 of February 1901), and judging from the various faces and lack of urgency, the train is returning home after a successful clearing up operation.

J. B. Hodgson Collection

ROYAL VISITS

These were always treated as an opportunity to show off the Company to its best advantage, and it was woe betide the railwayman who got things wrong.

Plate 269 (above) and 270 (overleaf) The new King, George V, and his wife Queen Mary, made a tour of Lancashire in July 1913. Having arrived at Blackpool by road on 8th July, their Majesties left Talbot Road Station for Rainford to lunch at Knowsley Hall. *Plate 269* shows a gleaming Hughes 4-6-0, No. 1514, especially provided with an eight wheel tender, waiting the arrival of the King and Queen at a very neat and clean Talbot Road. *Plate 270* shows the Royal couple about to board the 'Royal Train'. This is the LNWR 'Royal Train' and George Armitage, Chairman of the L&Y, walks with the King whilst Aspinall accompanies Queen Mary. Ashton Davies, later vice-president of the LMS, is on Armitage's left and, moving too quickly for the camera, Arthur Watson, then Superintendent of the line and later General Manager of the L&Y.

National Railway Museum

Plate 271   A view of all three engines involved in the 'Royal Train' movements on 9th July 1913. The train was to proceed from Rainford to Colne. Recently rebuilt 4-4-0, No. 1229 acted as 'Royal Pilot' and was driven by C. Burchall of Bolton shed, whilst the train itself was drawn by Hughes 4-6-0s. No. 1514, driven by W. Wing of Sandhills, was leading, and No. 1525, driven by J. Southworth of Blackpool, was the train engine. The finish on all three engines is superb and includes the burnishing of the smokebox ring on the 4-4-0.

National Railway Museum

Plate 272 The 'Royal Train' waiting at Rochdale for the return of the King and Queen who had taken a motor tour through East Lancashire from Colne to Rochdale. Whilst waiting at Rochdale, the men in charge of the train, drivers, guards, and senior station staff, had the opportunity to be photographed. The engines and vehicles have attracted a reasonable crowd of sightseers who are also eager for a glimpse of the King who is passing their homes.

National Railway Museum

Plate 273 The old frontage of Manchester Victoria *(see Plate 3)*, decorated for the visit of Edward VII in July 1905. This building was soon to disappear behind a new, and the present, facade and was eventually to be demolished to make way for the cafe at the north end of the concourse. Even the Prince of Wales's feathers, used on a previous Royal occasion, have been resurrected to add to the decorations.

National Railway Museum

THE GREAT WAR

At its zenith, the L&Y was to be greatly influenced by the 'War to end all wars', far more so than has been documented, by many railway historians, to date. Fortunately, the L&Y directors built up a very full photographic record of the events which affected the Railway. The ensuing photographs deal with locomotives, carriages, wagons, lurries, munitions, external influences and other various notable events which took place during this period. This is by no means a complete record, but just a small selection.

Plates 274 (above) and 276 (right)   A line up of a few of the thirty two 0-6-0s selected to go to France in 1917 is shown in *Plate 274*. They were fitted with drag chains and were given entirely new number-plates in a '1700' series. Their six wheel tenders were swapped for eight wheel ones borrowed from 0-8-0 locomotives. The engines were returned between April and September 1919. Nearest the camera is No. 1706 (formerly No. 92, Works No. 292 of April 1894, withdrawn in 1931 as LMS No. 12221) and No. 1712 (L&Y No. 1184, Works No. 195 of November 1892 and withdrawn in September 1948 as LMS No. 12170). For the remainder of their lives, the engines had front buffer beams with additional square holes cut into them. They are pictured in Horwich Works yard in December 1916. *Plate 276* is an enlargement of one of the special cast number-plates.

National Railway Museum

Plate 276

Plate 275   A most unfortunate looking wartime experiment to engine chimneys was when 0-6-0, No. 468 was fitted with a bent chimney made up from steel plates. The idea was to prevent engine smoke being seen by the enemy. The lack of success of this venture can be seen and the footplate staff had, no doubt, one or two choice phrases and comments. The locomotive was worked up and down the line on Sunday 23rd December 1916, and modifications were thought necessary. On 30th December it reappeared featuring a reversing rod especially for the chimney. This met with the same lack of success and the experiment was abandoned before it became too farcical.

National Railway Museum

Amongst other locomotive features during the Great War was the construction of ten additional saturated round top 0-6-0s featuring as many spare parts as could be found. These engines had narrow valances below the footplate. Some spare parts were also machined for Belgian engines but the exact types involved are unknown.

Plate 277 On the coaching scene, the War Office asked for several ambulance trains to be supplied at various intervals, and at least seven trains had L&Y origins. Train numbers 6 and 17, delivered in August 1914, were assembled from existing stock which was specially refurbished for the job. They ran only in Britain as nine coach sets but were later increased to ten or eleven vehicles. Of the trains for overseas use, Nos. 24 (delivered September 1915), and 29 (April 1916) were similarly composed of rebuilt stock, but each train comprised sixteen vehicles. Train No. 42, third in the overseas series, was built new and all three were painted drab with Geneva crosses. Finally, two trains of sixteen coaches each, Nos. 59 and 61, were built specifically for use by the American forces. On completion, it was common practice to take a new train from town to town for exhibition to the public and for fund raising. *Plate 277* shows part of train No. 29 at Blackburn on 12th February 1916. Six coaches are in the bay platform with No. 29L, a ward car with 36 beds, and No. 29F a pharmacy car and treatment room, being closest to the camera. Of great interest, too, are the various bits of station furniture, water towers, signal guys, etc. Eventually all the trains were returned and the vehicles were rebuilt and returned to normal traffic.

National Railway Museum

Plates 278 to 281 (below and overleaf) Four interior views displaying what was possible with the carriage builder's art. *Plate 278* shows the kitchen of No. 24 train (Coach 'A', formerly L&Y No. 573, a 54 ft. 0 in. five compartment brake). *Plate 279* is an infectious ward from the same train, complete with flowers. In *Plate 280*, the grisly looking operating table from No. 6 train is portrayed and *Plate 281* shows the pharmacy from No. 17 train (Coach 'A', formerly L&Y No. 1257, a 49 ft. 0 in. four compartment brake). Extensive use has been made of the fake tiling produced at that time and the bath and geyser have been slotted in very neatly.

National Railway Museum

Amongst other conversions carried out, some of the six wheel vehicles were turned into aeroplane vans for transporting planes in kit form and some were reduced to a mere chassis to carry the aeroplane bodies.

Plate 279

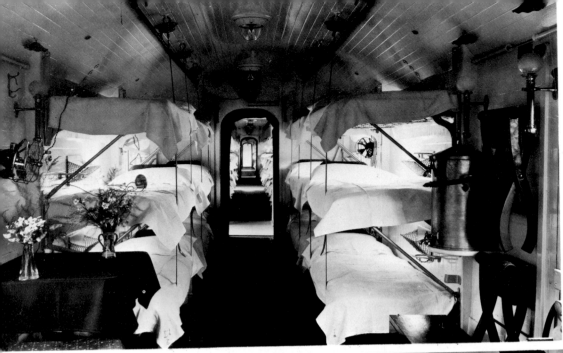

Plate 280

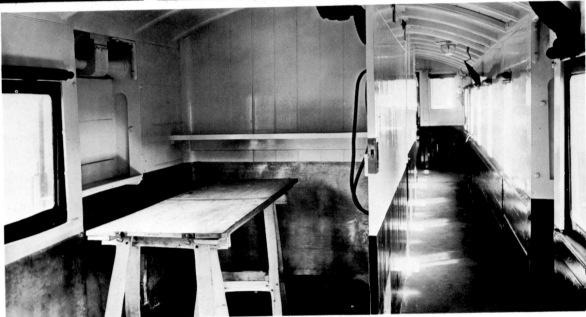

PHARMACY

Plate 281

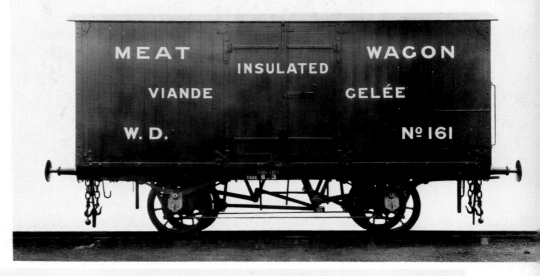

Plate 282 The use of wagon stock for the Great War fell into two categories; wagons built specifically for war service and those requisitioned from stock for overseas duties. This photograph shows one of the one hundred and fifty similar insulated vans built to Order E53 and paid for by the War Office. They bore little resemblance to contemporary L&Y styles but the ironwork, solebars and running gear are pure L&Y. The vans, 20 ft. 0 in. long, 8 ft. 2 in. wide and on a 10 ft. 6 in. wheelbase were seemingly destined for France. They were built late in 1915 but it is not known if any returned to Britain, although diagram book page 97, was kept open for them.

National Railway Museum

In addition to these, some rectanks were constructed and many covered goods wagons were altered for the conveyance of specialist materials, such as the Diagram 95 Picric acid vans.

Plates 283 and 284 For wagons taken out of traffic to go overseas, a general overhaul and repaint was required along with a new running number. Other special alterations included screw couplings and the packing out of the buffers. *Plate 283* shows L&Y No. 36002 from Diagram 63, a 21 ft. 6 in. long by 8 ft. 0 in. wide wagon with a 12 ft. 0 in. wheelbase, ready for the 'off' in January 1917. It is not known exactly how many wagons went overseas, but on several occasions fifty or so recently prepared open wagons, or single bolsters, were trundled out on to the line and photographed. *Plate 284* shows a similar Diagram 63 wagon as returned. This one has fared quite well and does not seem to have been knocked about much. Some were returned stripped of all wood or metal above the siderail whilst some five plank open wagons returned as single bolsters. All returnees were eventually overhauled and those without sides had them replaced but became fixed end vehicles in the process. WD No. 91867 has retained the L&Y number-plate, the only direct evidence of Company ownership but the L&Y characteristics of 'Load to be evenly distributed' plate and the style of tare weight remains. However, some foreign influences have been picked up en route and the wagon, L&Y No. 18548, was in an interesting form when photographed in April 1919.

National Railway Museum

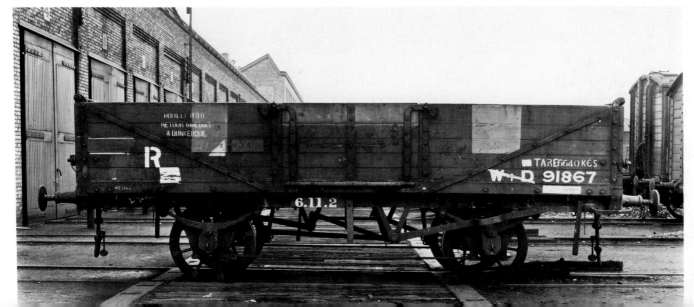

Plate 285 A considerable amount of the munitions work involved the building of many carts and service wagons for use in the field. Here, late in 1914, ten water carts are ready for shipment. Five dropside wagons of Diagram 15 are being used, the break is one of the older six wheelers from Diagram 43 and the engine is No. 288 (Works No. 736 of 11th March 1901, withdrawn as LMS No. 12423 in April 1937).

National Railway Museum

Plate 286 This photograph shows a light service wagon called for by the War Office in the late summer of 1914. Many existing drays were thus 'called up' and with minor modifications, such as reshafting for two horses, and a repaint, they were sent overseas. The scene is Newton Heath Works yard on 12th September 1914.

National Railway Museum

Plate 287 The Great War saw immense improvements in motor lorry design and the Leyland RAF type was manufactured in vast quantities. The L&Y supplied chassis from Horwich and bodies from Newton Heath and the War Office had hoped that they could build up to sixty units per week. This photograph shows a line of recently completed vehicles ready for overseas. Many were returned to the L&Y after the war and were dealt with as per *Plate 243*.

National Railway Museum

Plate 288 Some munitions work included the construction of guns or gun carriages. This is an 8 in. Howitzer recently completed at Horwich in August 1916. In the background all the paraphernalia of repairing locomotives still goes on.

National Railway Museum

Plate 289 Large quantities of shells of many types and sizes were assembled in Horwich Works. This is the cartridge case plant inside the boiler shop, late in 1916. The heavy influx of female labour, (*see also Plates 291 to 293*), is already apparent and the bench, which the girls are using, is made from old timbers and a tender side. On the original photograph it is also possible to identify a Company crest on the tender side.

National Railway Museum

Plate 290 One of the most interesting munition requisitions was for parts for a 2 ft. 0 in. gauge light railway, to be used just behind the 'Front'. This photograph shows the prefabricated point of an ingenious rivetted construction which came in three parts; blade, intermediate and frog, as well as having ready-made connections (as in a model railway). The balance weight is marked 'W ↑ D, LYR, 1917, and is photographed on 20th January 1917.

National Railway Museum

Plates 291 to 293   As men from the L&Y left their jobs and volunteered for the services, their places were taken by women. Fairly menial tasks were undertaken by them at first, but their duties later included more senior station positions, crane driving and minor engine repairs. *Plate 291* shows the cleaning out of a carriage of Oldham branch stock with the recessed door handle and the primitive vacuum cleaner is well worth noting. *Plate 292* shows a girl climbing up for a lamp inspection, the picture also giving a good view of the pipework and fittings attached to a headstock. *Plate 293* shows external cleaning, again on Oldham branch stock (Carriage No. 978 built to Diagram 66), with an ingenious plank device in use. *Plate 170* also shows female labour in an unexpected situation. Where clothing was concerned, mob-caps became commonplace and many ladies also had to wear trousers due to the nature of their work. At the end of the war some 5,500 women were on the Company payroll.

B. C. Lane Collection

Plate 294 Boys, too, were encouraged to help out. Here, five boys from Manchester Grammar School are unloading iron bars at Horwich Works. The wagon is from Diagram 63 and similar to those in *Plates 283 and 284*.

B. C. Lane Collection

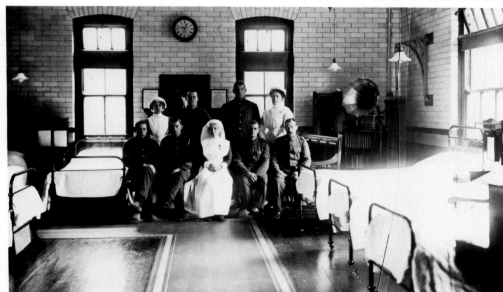

Plate 295 The L&Y was entrusted, via the Cottage Hospital, at Horwich Works with the care and treatment of wounded personnel. Originally built to accommodate infirm employees, the Cottage Hospital was situated next to the works. This photograph was taken in December 1914 when five privates and a corporal were convalescing. In the background, a standard signal bracket has been installed to allow those persons with severe breakages, but still with arm movement, a chance to pulley themselves to more comfortable positions.

National Railway Museum

Plate 296 The sad sight, repeated all over the country soon after the start of the Great War, was the entraining of horses destined for cartage behind the lines. The location is the goods yard at Ormskirk on 11th December 1914 as Army officers and Company servants organize the proceedings. The scene also displays the packed nature of many pre-group goods yards. Cattle van roofs were of bare wood with the gaps being tar-filled as no internal projections, such as nails being driven through, were allowed under RCH regulations.

National Railway Museum

TRIVIA AND MEMORABILIA

Like a great many companies, the L&Y stamped, gouged and identified its property from locomotive to tea cup. The origins of this practice were to prevent pilferage, especially of small items, although the L&Y did lay claim to being one of the few railways which had the misfortune to have a boiler stolen from a locomotive. E. L. Ahrons claimed that this event took place at Miles Platting Works during the 1860s when parts of a locomotive, awaiting attention, began to go missing, culminating, one night, in the disappearance of the whole boiler. Nevertheless, in later years, the L&Y was just as proudly proclaiming its property and these photographs show just a few of the many everyday items marked by the Company.

Plate 297

Plate 298

Plate 297　A letter rack and pen tray which was painted brown with white lettering and blue shading. Besides having 'L.Y.R. Co.' painted just above the pen tray handle, this letter rack has 'L&Y R' stamped on it twice, directly below the nail hole and on the pen tray itself.

G. Foxley Collection

Plate 298　A fish knife, using a garter design for identification. For some reason L&Y cutlery is somewhat rare.

B. C. Lane

Plate 299

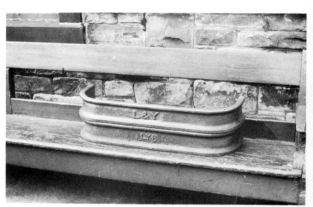

Plate 300

Plate 300　Two cast iron fenders photographed at Pleasington in the early 1960s. Two different styles were used by the L&Y.

E. Blakey

Plate 299　A privately preserved umbrella stand. This ornate item was to be found in waiting rooms. There should be a semicircular bar in front of the Company letters (L Y R), but its loss has allowed all the detail to be appreciated.

J. B. Hodgson

LANCASHIRE & YORKSHIRE RAILWAY.
Issued subject to the regulations and conditions in the Co's Time Tables, Books Bills & Notices Available on day of issue only.

FIRST   CLASS

TOTTINGTON To

On
L.&Y. RLY.

VIA

205   B.C.   ▲   FARE....s....d

6477

Plate 301 (above)　A 1st Class single ticket which was coloured white. Returns were yellow and white halves and there was a plethora of colours for the different classes and services offered. The best is reckoned to be a schoolboys' 3rd Class, twelve month season ticket which was three even sections of green, yellow and black.

G. H. Foxley

Plate 302 (right)　A cast iron gate bollard to prevent cart wheels catching the wooden gate post. This photograph, especially taken for this book at Accrington in March 1981, also demonstrates the sort of artefact still around sixty years after the passing of the L&Y.

N. G. Coates

Handbills were produced to advertise additional services and excursions. Aspinall realized the power of advertising and caused whole timetables, series of picture postcards, booklets of guided walks and other literature to be available for purchase, all in the hope of getting the public to buy a ticket. The L&Y also moved into the pictorial advertisement world, or poster field, and some interesting, though not artistically outstanding, examples were produced.

Plate 303 (below) A handbill of 1891 advertising 'Summer Saturday Excursions' and holidays to Southport.

B. C. Lane

Plates 304 and 305 (below) The extent to which companies would go to attract business is revealed in this 1910 advert printed in Yiddish to interest the large Manchester based Jewish community, and claimed to be inspired by Aspinall and A. Kaye-Butterworth. *Plate 305* pictures the translation into English.

J. B. Hodgson

Plate 306 An L&Y advertisement of 1912 destined for Germany. The flag is that of the East Coast Fleet, (blue and red quarters), and I will always be amused by the description of Aspinall as 'General Direktor'.

National Railway Museum

Plate 307 The exterior of Halifax Station on 30th August 1912, with the L&Y side displaying a fine collection of advertisements, both pictorial and informative. It has been possible to identify twenty one of the adverts shown, but space precludes their full description.

National Railway Museum

Plate 308 The use of running powers was quite widespread. Here, Midland 2-4-0, No. 142 pauses at Bolton in 1909 whilst working the 12.15 p.m. Blackburn to Chinley which included a through carriage to St. Pancras. There were many people who, when travelling between Blackburn and Bolton, preferred the plush Midland 3rd Class to the horsehair used on the L & Y.
D. F. Tee Collection

Plate 309 A Hoy 2-6-2T storms towards Stacksteads on the Bacup branch, a duty for which these particular engines were built.

Author's Collection

Plate 310 (below) A 2-4-2T, No. 31 heads up the Calder Valley with a stopping passenger train.

B. H. Ellston Collection

Plate 311 (above)   Aspinall 0-6-0 No. 1249 simmers in a
goods yard before moving on to its next stop. The loading
gauge is standard L&Y.

A. G. Ellis Collection

Plate 312 (right)   Large boilered 0-8-0, No. 408 sets out
from Manchester at the head of a long Yorkshire-bound
goods train.

The late G. W. Smith

Plate 312

Plate 313 (below)   During shunting duties, saddle tank No. 578 waits in the yard for the next rake of wagons. A merry looking crew and plate-
layer, with his flat hat and clogs, are all part of the daily scene on the L&Y.

J. B. Hodgson Collection

Plate 314   The L&Y officially lost its identity on 31st December 1921 and the ensuing twelve months were merely a mild flirtation with the LNWR, but with the formation of the LMS Railway on 1st January 1923, a whole new order came into being. By May, new livery styles and insignia were almost worked out and new locomotives began to bear the mark of the new company. Seen here is No. 1670, a Hughes 4-6-0, and every inch an L&Y engine, although the tender owed more to Great Central practice, being copied from the ROD type *(Plate 125)*. The date is 31st May 1923 and the engine is in L&Y passenger livery but clearly lettered 'LMS'. She was soon to become a red engine and carry the number 10441. The Hughes class plate is visible, Class 8 in this case, but the number-plate has changed slightly, now cast in steel with the legend reading 'L M & S Ry Co MAKERS' and 'HORWICH 1923'.

J. B. Hodgson Collection

Plate 315   To round off everything, a brake (LMS spelling). The black body, the yard plate, the rectangular number-plate and reporting number have all gone. The van is now in light grey, and a new number, 130,000 greater than its old one, is seen on a new plate and on the van side, but the tare weight is still in L&Y style. Newton Heath prepared this van for photographing on 4th May 1923.

National Railway Museum